THE PROPH

(Introduction of the Prophet)

Volume II

Printing Create Space (Amazon)

Special Thank You to Nikkia Ink, Inc. (Nicole Grace Williams) for editing and revising of manuscript.

This book is dedicated to my son and daughter Josiah and Miracle Sutton. I live my life, not only for those the Lord has called me to. But for my two precious angels I have the privilege of co-parenting. I don't know what I did to deserve you, but I know that you both have changed my life forever. As your dad, I pray that I can stand and make you proud. Both of you are the essence of who I am. My two young prophets, may the Lord guide you as you both grow in him and conquer the world that is ahead of you.

TABLE OF CONTENTS

Introduction

The Summons .... Chapter One

The Process .... Chapter Two

The Seven Laws of the Prophet .... Chapter Three

The Four Prophet's .... Chapter Four

The Placement .... Chapter Five

The Release .... Chapter Six

The Conclusion

In this second volume of The Prophet's Anatomy we will look to discover the identity of the prophet. This volume will speak to the heart of those searching to understand the prophet and the prophetic call. As you wrestle with the call, you will be faced with the choice to answer the call or to abandon the very life and thought of being the Lord's prophet. This volume provokes, challenges, and makes you think about the prophetic office in its entirety. You will be forced to look within yourself and ask what type of prophet am I? To whom am I called? And to what area of the prophetic am I called to operate? As you read this book, you will no longer be able to look at the prophetic office the same. When you take the journey to understand the prophetic office, bare in mind that you must be a student of the office. This literary work is made for those who seek to learn the ins and outs of the office. To evolve in the prophetic office of which God has called them, it will take a seeker, a passionate leader, and a learner. This book will give you revelation and place you on the path of becoming the prophet in which the Lord has called you. Be encouraged and know that after you have read this book you will know who you are and understand The Anatomy of the Prophet.

CHAPTER ONE

In Vol. I of "The Prophet's Anatomy" we discussed the reasons for which the Lord calls the prophet into service. This chapter will reiterate the reason and call of the prophet. As we understand the call of the prophet, we can pinpoint the experience of our own calling. The knowledge of that experience will help us to know God's mind in calling us as His prophets.

The "Narrative"

The prophetic call is a "narrative" which begins at the first revelation the Lord reveals to those he is calling into the prophetic ministry. The word "narrative" is defined by Webster Dictionary as, "a story or written account." For every prophet the Lord has sent into the earth has a *"narrative"* of his or her prophetic journey. The *"narrative"* is important. It tells the story of how the prophet came to be, his and her encounters with the Lord, their training, and assignment. The "narrative" is being built for the next prophet being called up to take the mantle of the prophet before him. The 21st Century is the last story of the prophets of old. They walked the earth and left the responsibility of the mantles behind, having realized that the prophets of today, aren't worthy to wear such a sacred garment. The problem we've encountered is that they have created their own anointing. Feeding on the greed of the culture and not prophets who possess the wisdom of the prophetic office. The mantles upheld by the prophets of old, told the stories of great battles of the spirit, movements that were birthed, and the revelation that shifted dispensation, culture and kingdoms.

Their "narratives" brought the church one step closer to the coming of our Lord and Savior Jesus Christ.

As you to continue to read this book, your challenge is to figure out your "narrative". Where did it begin? Which prophetic father plays a role to shape that "narrative"? And where do you stand today in that "narrative"? You ask, is this important? Yes! The task to know this is important. Your anointing, training, and who you'll become as a prophet depends on your ability to understand the narration of your prophetic journey. The "narrative" of the prophet's journey builds a mantle of relentless pursuit, pain and agony. It helps the prophet become a relentless force against the kingdom of darkness. Let's take a look at a familiar passage.

"As they were walking along and talking together, suddenly a chariot of fire and horses of fire appeared and separated the two of them and Elijah went up to heaven in a whirlwind. Elisha saw this and cried out, "My father! My father! The chariots and horsemen of Israel!" And Elisha saw him no more. Then he took hold of his garment and tore it in two. Elisha then picked up Elijah's cloak that had fallen from him and went back and stood on the bank of the Jordan. He took the cloak that had fallen from Elijah and struck the water with it. "Where now is the Lord, the God of Elijah?" He asked. When he struck the water, it divided to the right and to the left, and he crossed over. The company of the prophets from Jericho, who were watching, said, "The spirit of Elijah is resting on Elisha." And they went to meet him and bowed to the ground before him".
(2 Kings 2:11-15 NIV).

What we see in this passage is a prophet's "narrative" being carried on by the life of a young prophet who took the time to study and learn the "narrative" of the prophetic leader with whom he walked. Elisha's "narrative" began the moment he allowed Elijah's mantle to rest upon him, which was the day he left his father's house to become a servant to Elijah. Elisha never knew that his service to the Prophet Elijah would have him standing before the man of God awaiting a double portion of his spiritual father's spirit. What Elisha found was not only a double portion in his father's mantle, but his "narrative" was found in the mantle of Elijah. When the company of the prophet's look upon Elisha, and saw the "narrative" of Elijah they said, *"The spirit of Elijah is resting on Elisha." And they went to meet him and bowed to the ground before him. (2 Kings 2: 15 NIV)*

Elisha's "narrative" began when Elijah ended, yet Elijah's "narrative" was seen on the mantle of Elisha. When we understand that our "narrative" is developed and written for legacy, then, we will understand the importance of the prophetic mantle.

The Awakening

When the Lord summons the prophet, he must first awaken the prophet's spirit into his spirit. The Lord begins to provoke the prophet's dreams, visions, and intensifies the burning feeling in their hearts, hands and belly. They will feel the pain of others and will be burdened with deep passion of intercession. The prophet's ears will become keen. They will hear things that are incomprehensible and see what others can't see. The prophet will become agitated, moody and sensitive. They will become aggressive and isolate themselves from everyone. These acts of the calling will continue until the prophet answers the Lord's summon. The Lord will remain silent until the prophet responds. The following scripture depicts an experience between Yahweh, and the young Prophet Samuel.

One night Eli, whose eyes were becoming so weak that he could barely see, was lying down in his usual place. The lamp of God had not yet gone out, and Samuel was lying down in the house of the Lord, where the ark of God was. Then the Lord called Samuel.

Samuel answered, "Here I am." And he ran to Eli and said, "Here I am; you called me." But Eli said, "I did not call; go back and lie down." So he lay down. Again the Lord called, "Samuel!" And Samuel got up and went to Eli and said, "Here I am; you called me." "My son," Eli said, "I did not call; go back and lie down." Now Samuel did not yet know the Lord: The word of the Lord had not yet been revealed to him A third time the Lord called, "Samuel!" And Samuel got up and went to Eli and said, "Here I am; you called me."Then Eli realized that the Lord was calling the boy. So Eli told Samuel, "Go and lie down, and if he calls you, say, 'Speak, Lord, for your servant is listening.'" So Samuel lay down in his place. The Lord came and stood there, calling as at the other times, "Samuel! Samuel!"

Then Samuel said, "Speak, for your servant is listening." (1 Samuel 3:2-10, NIV)

What we see in 1 Samuel 3: 2-10 is the Lord's persistence in calling Samuel. Samuel's ears became keen on hearing a prophetic utterance. Samuel's awakening was in his ability to say yes Lord for "*... your servant is listening*". In doing so, he expressed his readiness in hearing the heart of the Revelator.

The Summons

Summons is translated in Hebrew as "Qara" which means invitation, order, reservation, calling or appointment. The word signifies something very significant.. It tells us that before the Lord place the prophet on the earth, he set a reservation for the prophet or he reserves the prophet for such an appointed time. The calling of the prophet was because the prophet had an appointment with the Lord. At such point in time, the summons was not a request, but an **"order."** In the Hebrew culture, when a king summons someone it was an honor and a sign of the king's recognition. The person had to respond quickly as the "order" was of utmost importance. Refusal of such an order brought forth death, the loss of property, and defilement of one's name among the court and throughout the land. The same applies when the Lord summons the prophet. It's an order to respond to the prophetic call and the prophet has a responsibility to respond. If the prophet refused to respond to the order, he or she have communicated that Yahweh was not to be honored or recognized. Not only would the refusal be a sign of disrespect, but it would hinder the appointed time of deliverance in which the Lord had set for his people. The following scripture describes such a deliverance.

"As the sun was setting, Abram fell into a deep sleep, and a thick and dreadful darkness came over him. Then the Lord said to him, "Know for certain that for four hundred years your descendants will be strangers in a country not their own and that they will be enslaved and mistreated there. But I will punish the nation they serve as slaves, and afterward they will come out with great possessions. You, however, will go to your ancestors in peace and be buried at a good old age. In the fourth generation your descendants will come back here, for the sin of the Amorites has not yet reached its full measure."(Genesis 15: 12-16, NIV).

In the book of Exodus 3: the Lord Summons Moses to fulfill such a prophecy:

The Lord said, "I have indeed seen the misery of my people in Egypt. I have heard them crying out because of their slave drivers, and I am concerned about their suffering. So I have come down to rescue them from the hand of the Egyptians and to bring them up out of that land into a good and spacious land, a land flowing with milk and honey—the home of the Canaanites, Hittites, Amorites, Perizzites,

Hivites and Jebusites. And now the cry of the Israelites has reached me, and I have seen the way the Egyptians are oppressing them. So now, go. I am sending you to Pharaoh to bring my people the Israelites out of Egypt."(Exodus 3: 7-10, NIV)

Moses' summons was ordered by the Lord to bring his people out of bondage. The prophetic word spoken in Genesis 15: 12-16 before Moses' birth was a sign of his appointment. Realize that when we are summoned to the prophetic office, the Lord has spoken prophetically on our lives before our birth. That summons is for us to come and hear the instruction of the Lord. A prophet, which is summoned to hear the instruction of the prophetic office will later be released to prophesy.

The prophet lies in wait, waiting to be called by the Lord. For it is the Lord's will to keep the prophet hidden until the proper time and season in which he has destined for that prophet to come forth. The prophet from the creation of the world was set apart.

In the book of Jeremiah we read one of the most famous scriptures written:

Before I formed you in the womb I knew you, before you were born I set you apart; I appointed you as a prophet to the nations." (Jeremiah 1:5 NIV)

The phrase "set apart" points to the sacredness of the prophet's life and assignment. But the word that stands out in the scripture is "Appointed", which has a synonym of the word "schedule" meaning a set time of appearance. The prophets coming through the spiritual matrix in this season must understand there is a time for their appearance. No prophet can take it upon themselves to come forth, be released from training, or prophesy until the appointed time. Many prophets of the 21st century have come forth before their appointed time. This quick manifestation has taken place because of the young prophet's desire to be popular. Rushing to create a ministry of the image rather than understanding the anatomy and the authenticity of the prophetic office. This has caused the young prophet to forsake being a student of the office. In the life of the prophetic, we see how the prophet must handle his or her awakening. Jesus in His development first became a student of the things of the Lord.

Scripture Excerpt: Book of Luke, John & Matthew

"When they did not find him, they went back to Jerusalem to look for him. After three days they found him in the temple courts, sitting among the teachers, listening to them and asking them questions. Everyone who heard him was amazed at his understanding and his answers. When his parents saw him, they were astonished. His mother said to him, "Son, why have you treated us like this? Your father and I have been anxiously searching for you." "Why were you searching for me?" He asked. "Didn't you know I had to be in my Father's house?" But they did not understand what he was saying to them. Then he went down to Nazareth with them and was obedient to them. But his mother treasured all these things in her heart. And Jesus grew in wisdom and stature, and in favor with God and man." (Luke 2:45-52, NIV)

We see from Jesus that his first step in his ministry is this image of him being a student. It is in his ability to be a student that grows in wisdom, stature and favor with God and man. For the young prophet coming up, he or she must understand the process of being a student. We will talk more about this in the chapter entitled, "The seven Laws of the Prophet." When Jesus learns to be a student, he waits eighteen years before he comes before John the Baptist. It is here he is "summoned" by the Lord. The Greek meaning of the word summons is to convene, assemble, order, call, or to announce. When John is at the Jordan River, baptizing the Jordan becomes more about the baptism. It also becomes the place where the Lord is convening and assembling His people so they may hear the order, the call and the announcement of Jesus. John with a loud voice said, *"Behold! The Lamb of God who takes away the sin of the world!" (John 1:29)* This announcement shows us Jesus' response to the prophetic call and the empowerment once he answered the call.

"And John bore witness, saying, "I saw the Spirit descending from heaven like a dove, and He remained upon Him. I did not know Him, but He who sent me to baptize with water said to me, 'Upon whom you see the Spirit descending, and remaining on Him, this is He who baptizes with the Holy Spirit.' And I have seen and testified that this is the Son of God." (John 1:32-34, NIV)

The summons revealed in this passage of scripture shows us something very important that has been lost among today's church culture. No one has borne witness of today's prophetic voices. Most so-called prophetic voices have been eliminated in heaven because they did not allow someone to bear witness of their prophetic call. Instead, they've risen to become false prophets. The false prophet is not defined by speaking false prophetic utterances. They never ordained to speak as no one having borne witness of their prophetic call. For the prophet to speak falsely is because he/she provoked the prophetic call before they were summoned, or they forsook the training by moving before their appointed time. Let me explain, the word false means something that is not true, real, and has not been authenticated or has not been validated. When a prophet does not answer the summons and goes through the proper protocol of someone bearing witness of his or her prophetic call, that prophet has risen falsely. He/She has now moved into the identity of a false prophet. Which means anything they prophesy are false because they were never released to do so. When John tried to stop Jesus from going through proper protocol, Jesus said to John "It should be done, for we must carry out all that God requires" (Matthew 3:15, NLT)

Today's prophets must understand that they cannot come forth until all the requirements set in place concerning their prophetic ministry is fulfilled. If a prophet has moved before these requirements are fulfilled, then they must not think that he/she has the spirit of the Lord on their prophetic mantle. For the spirit only empowers the prophetic mantle when the righteous requirements are fulfilled.

But Jesus said, "It should be done, for we must carry out all that God requires." So John agreed to baptize him. After his baptism, as Jesus came up out of the water, the heavens were opened and he saw the Spirit of God descending like a dove and settling on him. And a voice from heaven said, "This is my dearly loved Son, who brings me great joy."(Matthew 3:15-16, NLT)

CHAPTER TWO

The Process

When the prophet is awakened, the journey begins for an uphill battle for that prophet to become everything God intends for him or her. Their lives are now subject to what we know as prophetic process. Prophetic process is the process in which the prophet undergoes to have his or her prophetic sense and extremities developed. It is also the process in which the character of the prophet is brought out and dealt with. The prophetic process of the prophet may reign from one to twenty years. This depends on the prophet's obedience to the process and the reality they will face. For the prophet to understand the process, they must understand it is not about being perfect, but facing the reality of who you are and what is inside you.

For years budding prophets have forsaken the prophetic process for ego, fame and popularity. They have left their purpose on the table and have gone after images that will please the heart of humanity instead of the heart of God. When prophets enter this realm, it is because they have given up on the prophetic process. The prophetic process has never been easy and will not be easy until we embark upon heaven. The prophetic process is not only there to develop our prophetic sense, but also it is there to weed out the prophets who dare take upon this office without understanding the depth and sacred aspects of it. It is there for those who try to operate without understanding the power that lies in our prophetic sense. Those who try to take upon the prophetic office without prophetic process

rise only to becoming false in the eyes of God and His people.
The prophetic process begins with the senses of the prophet. These senses are the vehicles in which the Lord uses to display his power and authority to the lives of his people. The prophet that enters this process must understand that the full development of these senses must be the top priority of their office. In this chapter, the prophetic process is explained detailing what the prophet endures. The process of each sense is broken down to show you how the Lord developed the anatomy of the prophet using a different prophet of the Old Testament.

In "*The Prophet's Anatomy*" *VI*, "*The Anatomy*" I talk about the seven components that must go through the process in order to develop the prophet. The chapter entitled, *The Anatomy*, explains the necessity of each component. Here I will discuss the tedious process of all seven.

The Mind

"Then the Spirit lifted me up, and I heard behind me a great thunderous voice: "Blessed is the glory of the LORD from His place!" I also heard the noise of the wings of the living creatures that touched one another, and the noise of the wheels beside them, and a great thunderous noise. So the Spirit lifted me up and took me away, and I went in bitterness, in the heat of my spirit; but the hand of the LORD was strong upon me. Then I came to the captives at Tel Abib, who dwelt by the River Chebar; and I sat where they sat, and remained there astonished among them seven days." (Ezekiel 3:12-15 NKJV)

The mind of the prophet is a place of revelation. It becomes the center of the Lord's focus because the mind is the most significant part of the Lord getting his heart to his people. The prophet then must be able to handle the mental capacity of the revelation given to him/her by the Lord. The Lord then will spend years and months training the mind of the prophet, putting them through the depths of revelations, disturbing them through vision and dreams, and then not revealing nor opening their minds for months. The prophet at this point must journal the instructions given to him by Yahweh. As the prophet's mind is being awakened by the Lord, their mind is taken through the process of evolving and strengthening for service of the prophetic office. In Ezekiel 3:12-15 you see the prophet Ezekiel taken in the spirit and then coming out of it, only to be left by the River of Chebar in the bitterness and heat of his spirit. This is the process of the mind as it is being prepared to handle the revelation of the Lord.

The Ears

"Now the boy Samuel ministered to the LORD before Eli. And the word of the LORD was rare in those days; there was no widespread revelation. And it came to pass at that time, while Eli was lying down in his place, and when his eyes had begun to grow so dim that he could not see, and before the lamp of God went out in the tabernacle of the LORD where the ark of God was, and while Samuel was lying down, that the LORD called Samuel. And he answered, "Here I am!" So he ran to Eli and said, "Here I am, for you called me." And he said, "I did not call; lie down again." And he lay down. Then the LORD called yet again, "Samuel!" So Samuel arose and went to Eli, and said, "Here I am, for you called me." He answered, "I did not call, my son; lie down again." (Now Samuel did not yet know the LORD, nor was the word of the LORD yet revealed to him.) And the LORD called Samuel again the third time. So he arose and went to Eli, and said, "Here I am, for you did call me." Then Eli perceived that the LORD had called the boy. Therefore Eli said to Samuel, "Go, lie down; and it shall be, if He calls you, that you must say, 'Speak, LORD, for Your servant hears.' " So Samuel went and lay down in his place. Now the LORD came and stood and called as at other times, "Samuel! Samuel!" And Samuel

answered, "Speak, for Your servant hears." (I *Samuel 3:1-10, NKJV)*

The ear of the prophet is the place of guidance and instructions. The Lord trains the prophet's ear by giving constant instruction. These instructions train the prophet on obedience, detail and presentation. The prophet will learn the different voices of the Lord and how he speaks. They will be placed in different trials and asked to learn his voice in these trials. In moments of self-doubt, they will learn and begin to know the voice of the Lord. They must also be able to understand that their ears will be the place to help set free those the Lord has sent them to. The process of the prophet's ear depends on the future of someone they will encounter. Even after the prophet has matured his/her ear will still be under prophetic training.

And the word of the Lord came to him: "What are you doing here, Elijah?" He replied, "I have been very zealous for the Lord God Almighty. The Israelites have rejected your covenant, torn down your altars, and put your prophets to death with the sword. I am the only one left, and now they are trying to kill me too."
The Lord said, "Go out and stand on the mountain in the presence of the Lord, for the Lord is about to pass by." Then a great and powerful wind tore the mountains apart and shattered the rocks before the Lord, but the Lord was not in the wind. After the wind there was an earthquake, but the Lord was not in the earthquake. After the earthquake came a fire, but the Lord was not in the fire. And after the fire came a gentle whisper. When Elijah heard it, he pulled his cloak over his face and stood at the mouth of the cave.
Then a voice said to him, "What are you doing here, Elijah?"(1Kings 19:9-13, NIV)

The Eyes

"Moreover the word of the LORD came to me, saying, "Jeremiah, what do you see?" And I said, "I see a branch of an almond tree." Then the LORD said, "You have seen well, for I am ready to perform My word." And the word of the LORD came to me the second time, saying, "What do you see?" And I said, "I see a boiling pot, and it is facing away from the north." (Jeremiah 1:11-13 NKJV)

The Lord illuminates the prophet's eyes so they may see beyond the natural. The prophet's eyes are trained through years of learning how to see and discern the spirit of the Lord in a natural environment. The prophet must learn to see beyond the flaws of individuals and see whom the Lord has called them. The prophet must not allow the flaws of what is in the natural realm to keep them from seeing what is in the spirit realm. Jesus teaches us this with Peter when he called him Cephas the Rock. Shortly after, he sees Satan rise in him. The prophet must have this ability if he/she is to advance in their training. The Lord took Jeremiah the prophet outside and asked him what he saw! The Prophet must be able to see in the spirit realm. Being able to see in the spirit, is the essence of the prophet's mantle. If the prophet is unable to see in the spirit, then the prophet's natural sense still has him/her captive. In order for the prophet to rid his/herself of captivity, the prophet is required to spend hours, days, even months learning how to live in the spirit until their eyes are consumed by it. It is only then will they be able to see through the eyes of the spirit.

The Mouth

"In the year that King Uzziah died, I saw the Lord sitting on a throne, high and lifted up, and the train of His robe filled the temple. Above it stood seraphim; each one had six wings: with two he covered his face, with two he covered his feet,

and with two he flew. And one cried to another and said: "Holy, holy, holy is the LORD of hosts; The whole earth is full of His glory!" And the posts of the door were shaken by the voice of him who cried out, and the house was filled with smoke. So I said: "Woe is me, for I am undone! Because I am a man of unclean lips, And I dwell in the midst of a people of unclean lips; For my eyes have seen the King, The LORD of hosts." Then one of the seraphim flew to me, having in his hand a live coal, which he had taken with the tongs from the altar. And he touched my mouth with it, and said: "Behold, this has touched your lips; Your iniquity is taken away, And your sin purged." (*Isaiah 6:1-7, NKJV)*

The mouth is the prophet's weapon. It is a deadly, yet graceful component the prophet. The Lord uses the prophet's mouth to raise up and sit leaders down. He uses it to raise the dead yet bring destruction or blessing upon a city. He uses the prophet's mouth as an instrument to bless the people, yet shift the direction of their lives. It is the very bullet that can destroy the destiny of those around him/her. For this reason, the prophet's mouth must be purged. The prophet will be pressured by trials, tested by those around them, and pushed to the limits only to see how they will verbally respond. The Lord could spend years developing the mouth of a prophet so the importance of the tongue and how to use it is revealed. Blessings and curses lie in the mouth of a prophet. And the prophet must understand how to hostile his/her tongue when things don't go their way, when they meet opposition, and when the world is in chaos. The prophet must allow the spirit to completely guide his/her utterances. God created the spirit of the prophet for this reason and until the tongue goes through and is under complete spiritual submission, their prophetic authority will not be activated.

The Heart

"Now it came to pass after these things, that God tested Abraham, and said to him, "Abraham!" And he said, "Here I am." Then He said, "Take now your son, your only son Isaac, whom you love, and go to the land of Moriah, and offer him there as a burnt offering on one of the mountains of which I shall tell you." So Abraham rose early in the morning and saddled his donkey, and took two of his young men with him, and Isaac his son; and he split the wood for the burnt offering, and arose and went to the place of which God had told him. Then on the third day Abraham lifted his eyes and saw the place afar off. And Abraham said to his young men, "Stay here with the donkey; the lad and I will go yonder and worship, and we will come back to you." So Abraham took the wood of the burnt offering and laid it on Isaac his son; and he took the fire in his hand, and a knife, and the two of them went together. But Isaac spoke to Abraham his father and said, "My father!" And he said, "Here I am, my son." Then he said, "Look, the fire and the wood, but where is the lamb for a burnt offering?" And Abraham said, "My son, God will provide for Himself the lamb for a burnt offering." So the two of them went together. Then they came to the place of which God had told him. And Abraham built an altar there and placed the wood in order; and he bound Isaac his son, and laid him on the altar, upon the wood. And Abraham stretched out his hand and took the knife to slay his son." (Genesis 22:1-10 NKJV)

The heart of the prophet is the very engine that drives his/her mantle. It's constantly being tested through sacrifice. The mantle is driven by passion. A fire that will push the prophet through the hard times from the assignments given to them by Yahweh. The heart will reveal the very identity and obedience of the prophet. It speaks of their legacy. The heart of the prophet is processed to ensure they know who they are, and what they are prior to being exposed to their prophetic assignment. The Lord wanted to see Abraham's heart to know if Abraham's heart was connected with His heart. He tested Abraham to see if he could sacrifice the very thing he loved. From his selflessness and obedience, the Lord spared his son's life. Genesis 22:1-10 shows us, the heart of a prophet so connected with His God, he trusted him with the very thing he loved. Prophets, your heart will be the key that says you're ready.

The Hands

"So the LORD said to him, "What is that in your hand?" He said, "A rod." And He said, "Cast it on the ground." So he cast it on the ground, and it became a serpent; and Moses fled from it. Then the LORD said to Moses, "Reach out your hand and take it by the tail" (and he reached out his hand and caught it, and it became a rod in his hand), "that they may believe that the LORD God of their fathers, the God of Abraham, the God of Isaac, and the God of Jacob, has appeared to you." (Exodus 4:2-5 NKJV)

"But Jehoshaphat said, "Is there no prophet of the LORD here, that we may inquire of the LORD by him?" So one of the servants of the king of Israel answered and said, "Elisha the son of Shaphat is here, who poured water on the hands of Elijah."
(II Kings 3:11 NKJV)

The prophet's hand is the place of cultivating, building and evolving. It is the place of impartation and transformation. It is the place where signs and words take place. The hand of the prophet shows the work of the revealed heart of God. It releases the covenant of blessing; it releases the oil on those chosen to lead. The prophet's hands will speak of their service to those they have served and are serving. It speaks of their history and effectiveness on earth. It speaks of their value and their worth. Through the hands of the prophet being processed, kingdoms are taken down and dominions are subdued. Your hands carry the power of the spirit. The history of the Kingdom of God will be written by the prophet.

The Feet

"Then Moses said, "I will now turn aside and see this great sight, why the bush does not burn." So when the LORD saw that he turned aside to look, God called to him from the midst of the bush and said, "Moses, Moses!" And he said, "Here I am." Then He said, "Do not draw near this place. Take your sandals off your feet, for the place where you stand is holy ground." (Exodus 3:3-5, NKJV)

The prophet's feet represent their journey. They carry burdens and blessings of the prophetic journey. Upon the prophet's feet are the assignments and missions of the prophetic. Revelation and establishment of the prophetic are in their feet. It tells of their power and authority. The feet of the prophet speak of their dominion and the weight of glory they carry in their mantle. In the Hebrew culture, once a prophet steps into the home, blessings and honor were bestowed upon that home. If the prophet were rejected by that home, doom would be upon it. It is the responsibility of the prophet to understand; to be aware that they cannot travel any or everywhere. They must allow the spirit of the prophet to guide him/her to the place of mission and assignment. The moment a prophet stands in the Lord's presence, his feet become holy and his/her lives are no longer their own. The young aspiring prophet must understand the importance of their feet. A journey lies and waits in the feet of the prophet, which will shape their destiny.

The Character Phase

The Character of Time

The prophet's character will be put on display as they enter the prophetic process. Everything about you will be vetted as you struggle to become the Lord's prophet. Your time will be tested. You can spend time with your family only to be interrupted by your training. The interruption is a test of your ability to sacrifice and fulfill the assignment. The lead prophet will also test your attitude while being sensitive to the needs and wants of your family. The testing has nothing to do with neglecting your family or having a balance between home and church. But for you to understand the nature and burden of the prophetic call. When you enter the prophetic office you and your family's lives will be interrupted.

The Sexual Character

You will be tested sexually. If you think your sexual hormones are heightened now. It will be even more in the prophetic process. For those who are married the burden of this is easy. For everyone else, it poses some difficulty as temptations will frequently present themselves. Whether you're married or single, sexual struggles start from within. Most prophetic leaders will not admit this, but it's imperative that you're fully aware and prepared for the process. Even by my admittance of this during the writing of this book, will bring about stir and attraction from various demonic influences. You must be confident in yourself and your prophetic call. Be honest about your struggles. Many prophets fall prey to their lust, because they weren't honest with the Lord nor themselves. Being honest with oneself, will elevate you to a place of purity and maturity. David never realized his sexual struggle until after his rebuke for killing

Uriah to cover up the pregnancy of Bathsheba. The passage of scripture below speaks of the Prophet David struggle.

"O LORD, do not rebuke me in Your wrath, Nor chasten me in Your hot displeasure! For Your arrows pierce me deeply, And Your hand presses me down. There is no soundness in my flesh Because of Your anger, Nor any health in my bones Because of my sin. For my iniquities have gone over my head; like a heavy burden they are too heavy for me. My wounds are foul and festering Because of my foolishness. I am troubled, I am bowed down greatly; I go mourning all the day long. For my loins are full of inflammation, and there is no soundness in my flesh. I am feeble and severely broken; I groan because of the turmoil of my heart. Lord, all my desire is before You; and my sighing is not hidden from You. My heart pants, my strength fails me; as for the light of my eyes, it also has gone from me." Psalms 38:1-10 NKJV

"Have mercy upon me, O God, According to Your loving kindness; According to the multitude of Your tender mercies, Blot out my transgressions. Wash me thoroughly from my iniquity, and cleanse me from my sin. For I acknowledge my transgressions, and my sin is always before me. Against You, You only, have I sinned, and done this evil in Your sight— That You may be found just when You speak, and blameless when You judge. Behold, I was brought forth in iniquity, And in sin my mother conceived me. Behold, You desire truth in the inward parts, and in the hidden part You will make me to know wisdom. Purge me with hyssop, and I shall be clean; Wash me, and I shall be whiter than snow. Make me hear joy and gladness that the bones You have broken may rejoice." Psalms 51:1-8

The Season of Character

Every prophet must deal with the season of waiting. While you are in prophetic process you will go through seasons of drought, spiritually, emotionally and financially. You will reach moments of breaking points and spiritual fatigue. You will go through seasons where you just have enough to pay your bills, and no more. While you are in the season of washing the prophet's hand, those around you will be a blessing. The worst thing you can do is not understand the season you are in and not know how that season relates to your prophetic office. You must understand everything about you being a prophet in this season. If you do not learn how to walk in the spirit of patience, you will question the season. Becoming bitter about the season and then moving out of process to get what you desire. This happened with the young trainee Gehazi. He moved out of his season wanting things he was not ordained to have. See scripture below.

"But Gehazi, the servant of Elisha the man of God, said, "Look, my master has spared Naaman this Syrian, while not receiving from his hands what he brought; but as the LORD lives, I will run after him and take something from him." So Gehazi pursued Naaman. When Naaman saw him running after him, he got down from the chariot to meet him, and said, "Is all well?" And he said, "All is well. My master has sent me, saying, 'Indeed, just now two young men of the sons of the prophets have come to me from the mountains of Ephraim. Please give them a talent of silver and two changes of garments.' " So Naaman said, "Please, take two talents." And he urged him, and bound two talents of silver in two bags, with two changes of garments, and handed them to two of his servants; and they carried them on ahead of him. When he came to the citadel, he took them from their hand, and stored them away in the house; then he let the men go, and they departed. Now he went in and stood before his master. Elisha said to him, "Where did you go, Gehazi?" And he said, "Your servant did not go anywhere." Then he said to him, "Did not my heart go with you when the man turned back from his chariot to meet you? Is it time to receive money and to receive clothing, olive groves and vineyards, sheep and oxen, male and female servants?"

II Kings 5:20-26 NKJV

Gehazi allowed himself to get caught up in the desires of his own flesh. He forsook the prophetic process chasing after material things. It's not that he couldn't have material things. The timing was not right for him to have them. It was not the right season. The prophetic process manifested the character of Gehazi and revealed his inability to handle the prophetic assignment and his inability to understand seasons.

The season of Stewardship and Faithfulness

Every prophet must prove himself or herself to be faithful and good stewards of what the Lord will place in their hands. We live in a dispensation were prophets have forsaken the prophetic process that will prove their faithfulness and stewardship of the assignment and anointing of the prophetic office. Such neglect on these prophets part has proven a character of self. This is dangerous because such a prophet will not seek what is best for the Lord's people, but what he or she wants. The prophet must show a character of service, commitment and justice. They must be ready to lay down their lives for a cause greater than themselves. If a prophet is not willing to do this, then that prophet has displayed an action and image that does not reflect the creative makeup of *The Prophets Anatomy*. The prophet will be recognized by their faithfulness and stewardship of what did not belong to them, but to someone else. His/Her faithfulness and stewardship is tied into their ability to understand what prophetic service is truly. This needs to be written upon the prophet's heart. The prophet must prove that he/she can serve by being an aide to the lead prophet in their life by assisting with tasks that would develop the prophetic ministry before them. That service should not only be a service to the man or woman of God, but to all people. While you are being faithful in the work of the prophetic ministry, realize and know the ministry you're helping establish, is not your own. It's another man's work which requires you to be diligent and faithfulness. We see this with the young prophets in their help to build the training facility of the prophets. Each prophet was required to bring their own beam, but use an ax that belong to another prophet:

"And the sons of the prophets said to Elisha, "See now, the place where we dwell with you is too small for us. Please, let us go to the Jordan, and let every man take a beam from there, and let us make there a place where we may dwell." So he answered, "Go." Then one said, "Please consent to go with your servants." And he answered, "I will go." So he went with them. And when they came to the Jordan, they cut down trees. But as one was cutting down a tree, the iron ax head fell into the water; and he cried out and said, "Alas, master! For it was borrowed." So the man of God said, "Where did it fall?" And he showed him the place. So he cut off a stick, and threw it in there; and he made the iron float. Therefore, he said, "Pick it up for yourself." So he reached out his hand and took it." (II Kings 6:1-7, NKJV)

The ax head lost by the young prophet did not belong to him, but to someone else. The young prophet knew that losing the ax head exposed his inability to handle the work of the prophetic ministry. The ax fell in the Jordan, which were deep waters. There was no way of getting it back unless he was guided by a prophetic gift stronger than his own. The prophet Elisha was teaching the young prophet something in his service. He was taught how to retrieve what was lost. No matter how something or someone had fallen into something deeper, it could be recovered by understanding the prophetic mantle. The young prophet could learn this because he realized there was someone with the ability to teach him how to stay faithful in service and to be a good steward of all things.

When prophets understand that everything about whom they are and what their prophetic ministry will become lies in their ability to serve, then many will recognize them. Only when the prophet recognizes that greatness is in their ability to be faithful, being a good steward, and of good service, will they see the fullness of their prophetic mantle.

"But Jehoshaphat said, "Is there no prophet of the LORD here, that we may inquire of the LORD by him?" So one of the servants of the king of Israel answered and said, "Elisha the son of Shaphat is here, who poured water on the hands of Elijah.""
(II Kings 3:11, NKJV)

As we concluded this chapter, let us not forget these seven components of the Prophets Anatomy. It defines our existence within the prophetic office. The very process of our character will become present. We then must understand that the prophetic process is not something we must take lightly, but it must be something we must embrace if we are to become the prophet the Lord created us to be. We should not look to forsake such a process, but run with it as we are the voice of the past, present and future. What we do in this hour, season and moment has everything to do with how we come out of prophetic process. For without prophetic process, the mantle which lies before us cannot and will not be empowered.

THE SEVEN LAWS OF THE PROPHET

CHAPTER THREE

The Seven Laws of the Prophetic Office

Most prophets don't understand there are rules to their mantle. These rules are not there to keep the prophet in bondage, but to help the prophet understand who he or she is in the times of trouble, the days of danger and in the moment of weakness. These laws will reveal the prophet's character. Challenging them to never forget their charge. It ensures the growth of the prophet helping to shape prophetic revelation in their mantle.

The seven laws presented to you today are valuable to the future development of such prophets that will come behind today's prophet. They are rules that will bring blessing, shape conviction and remind you of the heart of the prophet. These laws have not been concocted. They are rules given by the scriptures that lays the foundation for the prophet's mantle. Knowing these seven rules, will teach us how to act and fulfill our assignment.

The Law of Sacrifice

"So he departed from there, and found Elisha the son of Shaphat, who was plowing with twelve yoke of oxen before him, and he was with the twelfth. Then Elijah passed by him and threw his mantle on him. And he left the oxen and ran after Elijah, and said, "Please let me kiss my father and my mother, and then I will follow you." And he said to him, "Go

back again, for what have I done to you?" So Elisha turned back from him, and took a yoke of oxen and slaughtered them and boiled their flesh, using the oxen's equipment, and gave it to the people, and they ate. Then he arose and followed Elijah, and became his servant."
(I Kings 19:19-21 NKJV)

The law of prophetic sacrifice is the core belief that a prophet lives his or her life always ready to give up something for the prophetic mission. The prophet must always understand this if the prophet is to live in the full abundance of their prophetic mantle. The prophet must never get comfortable with that which is material, nor that which is relational. The prophet is always moving and shifting to different places, moments and seasons. With that changes are always occurring and the mission is always the center focus of the prophet's assignment. For Abraham it was giving up Ishmael, for Moses it was leaving his family behind, for Jeremiah it was not getting married in his own country, for Elisha it was leaving and inheritance behind and for Jesus it was having nowhere to lay his head. See the sacrifice is different for every prophet, but make no mistake every prophet must sacrifice. For this is the first rule of the prophet, this makes them who they are. You will cry many of nights because of this rule and you will have limited friends because of it. . Live your life always on the altar, but know there is a blessing that follows you. You will have much because your sacrifice and you will get double for what you have given up. Elisha ability to sacrifice for the prophetic call brought him into great power and lead him to do great things. He became a prophetic legend and his name written among the greatest.

The Law of the Student

"Now so it was that after three days they found Him in the temple, sitting in the midst of the teachers, both listening to them and asking them questions. And all who heard Him were astonished at His understanding and answers." (Luke 2:46-47 NKJV)

"And Jesus increased in wisdom and stature, and in favor with God and men."
(Luke 2:52 NKJV)

The prophetic mantle is forever evolving because of the ongoing revelation from the Lord. This means the prophet must be in a seat where they are learning and understanding what that revelation means and how it relates to the church, the Lord's people and the world. The Prophet must be able to increase in the wisdom of this revelation because it is vital to the growth of the Lord's people, the church and the work of ministry. If the prophet forsakes the seat of the student, then prophet has lost sight of the revelation given by the Lord and the mission and assignment he or she is on becomes hinder because he or she has forsaken the seat of the student. This means the church does not get what the Lord has revealed in its proper time, nor does the person who the Lord has sent the prophet to. The seat of the student must forever be sought by the prophet, for it is the place where the revelation of the Lord is revealed.

The Law of a Servant

"But Jehoshaphat said, "Is there no prophet of the LORD here, that we may inquire of the LORD by him?"

So one of the servants of the king of Israel answered and said, "Elisha the son of Shaphat is here, who poured water on the hands of Elijah." (II Kings 3:11 NKJV)

Everything about the future identity of the prophet is in their ability to understand the law of the servant. A prophet's name is known by his or her service to the man or woman of God before them. They are sought after, not because of their ability to prophesy, but because of their ability to get their hands dirty. The prophet must never think that the prophetic office is about him or her, but about the people the Lord sends that prophet too. The prophet learns the humility of his or her mantle in the service of the prophet who train them. A prophet who has not been trained in serving another is more likely going to move by the fame, popularity and prosperity that comes to the office. The prophet must learn that they are there to serve and not take from the Lord's people. They must never lose the towel that has been placed in their hands. Serving is a major responsibility of the prophet it is the reason for the process of their hands. The legacy of a prophet will not be because they prophesied to thousands, but because they left behind a legacy of serving.

The Law of Honor

"Then the men of David said to him, "This is the day of which the LORD said to you, 'Behold, I will deliver your enemy into your hand, that you may do to him as it seems good to you.' " And David arose and secretly cut off a corner of Saul's robe. Now it happened afterward, that David's heart troubled him because he had cut Saul's robe. And he said to his men, "The LORD forbid that I should do this thing to my master, the LORD's anointed, to stretch out my hand against him, seeing he is the anointed of the LORD." So David restrained his servants with these words, and did not allow them to rise against Saul. And Saul got up from the cave and went on his way."
I Samuel 24:4-7 NKJV

The Law of honor has been missing from the prophet's mantle. Most think that they may do whatever they want to whomever they want without consequence or repercussions. This is not the case for the prophet's mantle. Their mantle is created in the rule of honor. When the prophet is not honored then the anointing which he or she is called to serve becomes a target for the forces of darkness to penetrate and defeat the one anointed by God. The prophet must remember that honor protects the anointing, not the wrong or offense of the one anointed by God. The prophet must be wise in how he or she deal with such wrong or offense as the honor of that leader or person will set the tone for others around the prophet. The prophet must understand that honor is the difference between the prophet finishing an assignment or being benched by the Lord. It is an illegal act of heaven for a prophet to dishonor those in leadership or those under him/her and become a tyrant against them. The honor of a prophet will preserve the character of that prophet and the people that follow them. Without honor that prophet is nothing more than an evil agent of darkness, who has no respect for what the Lord has created. The Law of honor must be the written letter across the prophet chest. For it will speak of the heart of the prophet.

The Law of Prayer

"And Samuel said, "Gather all Israel to Mizpah, and I will pray to the LORD for you.""
(I Samuel 7:5 NKJV)

"Now there was one, Anna, a prophetess, the daughter of Phanuel, of the tribe of Asher. She was of a great age, and had lived with a husband seven years from her virginity; and this woman was a widow of about eighty-four years, who did not depart from the temple, but served God with fasting and prayers night and day." Luke 2:36-37 NKJV

The Law of Prayer is the foundational structure of the prophet's mantle. No prophet can engage in prophecy, warfare or sign and wonders without toiling in the agony of prayer. Prayer is the very weapon the prophet uses to prepare him or herself for the journey of ministry. In prayer the prophet connects and builds his or her relationship with God. In prayer the revelation of the Lord is released to the prophet. Even those around the prophet can feel such revelation happening. The prophet must know that his or her responsibilities is not only to spend countless hours in prayer, but to build prayer altars in their very placements and leading the people of the Lord in prayer. There is no prophet who could stand before the Lord's people without having spent the time in prayer. A prophet without prayer is like a whale without water, it simply cannot survive. If the prophet tries to engage in any act of ministry without spending time in prayer that prophet will be in danger of producing false revelation and leading a people down the wrong road. The prophet then must understand that the law of prayer is vital to his or mantle and the people they are called to speak to.

The Law of Covenant

"When Abram was ninety-nine years old, the LORD appeared to Abram and said to him, "I am the Almighty God; walk before Me and be blameless. And I will make My covenant between Me and you, and will multiply you exceedingly."

"As for Me, behold, My covenant is with you, and you shall be a father of many nations. No longer shall your name be called Abram, but your name shall be Abraham; for I have made you a father of many nations. I will make you exceedingly fruitful; and I will make nations of you, and kings shall come from you. And I will establish My covenant between Me and you and your descendants after you in their generations, for an everlasting covenant, to be God to you and your descendants after you. Also I give to you and your descendants after you the land in which you are a stranger, all the land of Canaan, as an everlasting possession; and I will be their God." And God said to Abraham: "As for you, you shall keep My covenant, you and your descendants after you throughout their generations. This is My covenant which you shall keep, between Me and you and your descendants after you: Every male child among you shall be circumcised; and you shall be circumcised in the flesh of your foreskins, and it shall be a sign of the covenant between Me and you. He who is eight days old among you shall be circumcised, every male child in your generations, he who is born in your house or bought with money from any foreigner who is not your descendant. He who is born in your house and he who is bought with your money must be circumcised, and My covenant shall be in your flesh for an everlasting covenant." Genesis 17:1-2, 4-13 NKJV

The prophet's ministry is built on a prophetic covenant between him and Yahweh. That covenant is important to the Lord as the prophet whole ministry is governed by that covenant. Not only is the prophetic covenant important to the prophet, but the covenant Yahweh has made with his church. For that reason, the prophet will be aggressive, picky and focused. They will never turn to the right or left because the covenant has Jesus blood on it. The covenant for the prophet carries meaning. It is defined by sacrifice and sign in holy blood. It speaks of redemption. A prophet will dare not allow anyone to treat the covenant establish as common. They understand the meaning of the covenant given to the church. The prophet is sent because the covenant has been broken. When the prophet comes, his or her assignment is to make sure that covenant remains enact, this why the prophet must understand the importance of his or her mantle. When it is all said and done the prophet must make sure that what remains is the covenant and how that covenant is established.

The Law of Order

"Now the word of the LORD came to Samuel, saying, "I greatly regret that I have set up Saul as king, for he has turned back from following Me, and has not performed My commandments." And it grieved Samuel, and he cried out to the LORD all night. So when Samuel rose early in the morning to meet Saul, it was told Samuel, saying, "Saul went to Carmel, and indeed, he set up a monument for himself; and he has gone on around, passed by, and gone down to Gilgal." Then Samuel went to Saul, and Saul said to him, "Blessed are you of the LORD! I have performed the commandment of the LORD." But Samuel said, "What then is this bleating of the sheep in my ears, and the lowing of the oxen which I hear?" And Saul said, "They have brought them from the Amalekites; for the people spared the best of the sheep and the oxen, to sacrifice to the LORD your God; and the rest we have utterly destroyed." Then Samuel said to Saul, "Be quiet! And I will tell you what the LORD said to me last night." And he said to him, "Speak on." So Samuel said, "When you were little in your own eyes, were you not head of the tribes of Israel? And did not the LORD anoint you king over Israel? Now the LORD sent you on a mission, and said, 'Go, and utterly destroy the sinners, the Amalekites, and fight against them until they are consumed.' Why then did you not obey the voice of the LORD? Why did you swoop down on the spoil, and do evil in the sight of the LORD?" And Saul said to Samuel, "But I have obeyed the voice of the LORD, and gone on the mission on which the LORD sent me, and brought back Agag king of Amalek; I have utterly destroyed the Amalekites. But the people took of the plunder, sheep and oxen, the best of the things which should have been utterly destroyed, to sacrifice to the LORD your God in Gilgal." So Samuel said: "Has the LORD great delight in burnt offerings and sacrifices, As in obeying the voice of the

LORD? Behold, to obey is better than sacrifice, And to heed than the fat of rams. For rebellion is as the sin of witchcraft, And stubbornness is as iniquity and idolatry. Because you have rejected the word of the LORD, He also has rejected you from being king." Then Saul said to Samuel, "I have sinned, for I have transgressed the commandment of the LORD, and your words, because I feared the people and obeyed their voice. Now therefore, please pardon my sin, and return with me, that I may worship the LORD." But Samuel said to Saul, "I will not return with you, for you have rejected the word of the LORD, and the LORD has rejected you from being king over Israel." And as Samuel turned around to go away, Saul seized the edge of his robe, and it tore. So Samuel said to him, "The LORD has torn the kingdom of Israel from you today, and has given it to a neighbor of yours, who is better than you. And also the Strength of Israel will not lie nor relent. For He is not a man, that He should relent." Then he said, "I have sinned; yet honor me now, please, before the elders of my people and before Israel, and return with me, that I may worship the LORD your God." So Samuel turned back after Saul, and Saul worshiped the LORD. Then Samuel said, "Bring Agag king of the Amalekites here to me."

So Agag came to him cautiously. And Agag said, "Surely the bitterness of death is past." But Samuel said, "As your sword has made women childless, so shall your mother be childless among women." And Samuel hacked Agag in pieces before the LORD in Gilgal." (I Samuel 15:10-33 NKJV)

The prophet never loses sight of his or her prophetic mission. They understand that the instructions given by the Lord must be carried out in the way God said it, how he said it, when he said it. This is the Law of order for the prophet. The prophet will come on scène instructing those whom the Lord has chosen. The prophet will look for those instructions, as they understand that a people, region or nation depends on the order of those instructions. The above passage of scripture speaks of this very thing as Samuel has given Saul instruction only to find that Saul did not carry out the instructions of the Lord. At that moment Samuel stood up to clean the mess up that Saul fell to take responsibility for. Samuel grabs a sword and kills everything Saul was commanded to kill. In all honesty, the prophet must have a heart for order. Without order the prophet sees rebellion and witchcraft. For the prophet this sense of darkness must be stopped at the church, the Lord's people and a generation depends on it. Today's prophet then must understand that order must be the very thing that captivates their heart. The prophet must look for order in everything he or she does. Without order, instructions from the Lord will go undone and the earth and a person will shake, because such order has been overlooked. If the prophet is to operate in the capacity of the prophetic office, then that prophet must understand the Law of order. For without order the kingdom of darkness will fulfill its purpose.

The Seven Laws present are not laws given to be major quotes that inspire the prophet. But they are the reality of which the prophet must learn and understand. The prophet cannot engage in his or her ministry ignorant of the Laws, which govern their mantle. They must adhere to these as the life of those they are called to depend on them understanding such laws that will define the future of the church, the Lord's people and generations. As the prophet seeks to understand these rules and allow them to be written on his and her heart, then the prophet will see the fruit of his or her labor as they establish the kingdom of God.

CHAPTER FOUR

The Four Prophets

As we look at the prophet's office one must be able to define the prophet and be able to see where they fit in the prophet's office. Today's prophets have come forth thinking they all are the same. This is because most prophets cannot define the prophet and the history in which the prophet has come about. Most don't understand the creative makeup of the prophet and the design in which the Lord has attended the prophet to look like. The Hebrew Bible describes four Hebrew words for the word prophet. These four words give us four images of the prophet and the Lord's creative purpose in which he wants to use the prophet in the earth.

What most prophets in the 21st century don't understand is that the Lord creates these four images of the prophet to bring forth the identity of the full makeup of the prophet. Each person called into the prophet's office make-up the totality of the prophet's anatomy in which the Lord embedded in the Holy Scripture. Everything about these four images is a mystery only unlock when the prophet is called, awaken and process. These four images have been lost in the greed, manipulation and deception of today's prophetic office. Young prophets have awakened only to come forth with the idea that every prophet is the same and each prophet carries the same creative makeup and mission. This idea has caused prophets to be in error, lost, and rebel against the divine will of the Lord. This has caused people in the church to be hurt by such prophets. Those prophets that are coming up have been hurt and they have no understanding of what today's prophet should look like. I have written this chapter to bring understanding of these four images so those that have been called and those walking in the prophet's office for years will find themselves and their placement in the earth.

The Four Types of Prophets

The Nabi

The word Nabi is one of the Hebrew words for the word prophet. It means to bubble forth, like a fountain. While most would look at the Nabi as a spokesman for God. There is a deeper meaning of this prophet as the Hebrew verb to bubble forth like a fountain, suggest this prophet carries the burden of intercession and the ability to bring forth the hidden mysteries of the Lord.

"And Samuel said, "Gather all Israel to Mizpah, and I will pray to the LORD for you." So they gathered together at Mizpah, drew water, and poured it out before the LORD. And they fasted that day, and said there, "We have sinned against the LORD." And Samuel judged the children of Israel at Mizpah. Now when the Philistines heard that the children of Israel had gathered together at Mizpah, the lords of the Philistines went up against Israel. And when the children of Israel heard of it, they were afraid of the Philistines. So the children of Israel said to Samuel, "Do not cease to cry out to the LORD our God for us, that He may save us from the hand of the Philistines." And Samuel took a suckling lamb and offered it as a whole burnt offering to the LORD. Then Samuel cried out to the LORD for Israel, and the LORD answered him. Now, as Samuel was offering up the burnt offering, the Philistines drew near to battle against Israel. But the LORD thundered with a loud thunder upon the Philistines that day, and so confused them that they were overcome before Israel. And the men of Israel went out of Mizpah, and pursued the Philistines, and drove them back as far as below Beth Car. Then Samuel took a stone and set it up between

Mizpah, and Shen, and called its name Ebenezer, saying, "Thus far the LORD has helped us." So the Philistines were subdued, and they did not come any more into the territory of Israel. And the hand of the LORD was against the Philistines all the days of Samuel. Then the cities which the Philistines had taken from Israel were restored to Israel, from Ekron to Gath; and Israel recovered its territory from the hands of the Philistines. Also, there was peace between Israel and the Amorites. And Samuel judged Israel all the days of his life. He went from year to year on a circuit to Bethel, Gilgal, and Mizpah, and judged Israel in all those places. But he always returned to Ramah, for his home was there. There he judged Israel, and there he built an altar to the LORD." (I Samuel 7:5-17 NKJV)

Samuel life gives us a picture of what the Nabi prophet looks like. He carries the burden of intercession, the heart of leadership and the ability to lead the Lord's people in repentance and deliverance. The prophet Samuel is the blueprint for such a prophet as the Nabi because his focus is on making sure the people understand the ways of Yahweh and what he expects from them. The Nabi prophet is so in tune with the covenant of Yahweh, the scariness of the house of the Lord, and the character of the leadership chosen by Yahweh. Such a prophet does not delight in the opinions of man, but the utterance of the Lord. The Nabi prophet must make sure that what the Lord has uttered is established. They become so burdened with the responsibility of making sure this happens that hindering such instruction will irritate the prophet causing him/her to act in the authority of their mantle. In 1 Samuel 13:5-14 we read such an act among the Prophet Samuel it reads:

"Then the Philistines gathered together to fight with Israel, thirty thousand chariots, and six thousand horsemen, and people as the sand which is on the seashore in multitude. And they came up, and encamped in Michmash, to the east of Beth Aven. When the men of Israel saw that they

were in danger (for the people were distressed), then the people hid in caves, in thickets, in rocks, in holes, and in pits. And some of the Hebrews crossed over the Jordan to the land of Gad and Gilead. As for Saul, he was still in Gilgal, and all the people followed him trembling. Then he waited seven days, according to the time set by Samuel. But Samuel did not come to Gilgal; and the people were scattered from him. So Saul said, "Bring a burnt offering and peace offerings here to me." And he offered the burnt offering. Now it happened, as soon as he had finished presenting the burnt offering, that Samuel came; and Saul went out to meet him, that he might greet him. And Samuel said, "What have you done?" Saul said, "When I saw that the people were scattered from me, and that you did not come within the days appointed, and that the Philistines gathered together at Michmash, then I said, 'The Philistines will now come down on me at Gilgal, and I have not made supplication to the LORD.' Therefore I felt compelled, and offered a burnt offering." And Samuel said to Saul, "You have done foolishly. You have not kept the commandment of the LORD your God, which He commanded you. For now the LORD would have established your kingdom over Israel forever. But now your kingdom shall not continue. The LORD has sought for Himself a man after His own heart, and the LORD has commanded him to be commander over His people, because you have not kept what the LORD commanded you.""" *(I Samuel 13:5-14 NKJV)*

The Nabi prophet rigors passion is never settled until what is spoken by the Lord has come to past. They have always sensed the urgency to make sure that what has been revealed is established. They possess a heart of administration, structure, order and development. They will never bypass these things to please man. These things will become the tools they use to set the prophetic word into motion. They would look for these things in the house of the Lord. If these things are missing, the prophet becomes engaged in doing what is necessary to restore order. The above reference of scripture shows us through the Prophet Samuel, the totality of Nabi prophet and what it looks like among the four design prophets.

The Roeh

The "Roeh" prophet is a prophet like no other it is defined in Hebrew terms as, "to see" or "to perceive". It speaks of one who reveals secrets or one who envisions. The Roeh prophet unlike the Nabi sees things in the spirit. Everything about this prophet is their ability to go in and out of the spirit. To establish those things in which they have seen or envisioned. While Nabi focuses on the utterance, the Roeh focuses on what has been seen in the spirit. The Roeh understands the shifting of the seasons, the understanding of dreams, and the culture of spiritual truths. The Roeh is always in the spirit. Being in the spirit realm enables the prophet to speak of future events and interpret dreams. The Roeh's job is to make sure that the imagery of heaven and the heart of God is established in the earth realm. The Roeh exposes hidden secrets, unseen warfare and divine dreams given to humanity. The Roeh has the ability to tap into the depths of man's heart. Exposing those secrets, whether good or bad. The bible presents to us such a prophet in Ezekiel. The prophet Ezekiel shows us the identity of the Roeh prophet. In the book of Ezekiel chapter 37:1-14 we see the blueprint of how the Roeh prophet is seen and operates;

"The hand of the Lord was on me, and he brought me out by the Spirit of the Lord and set me in the middle of a valley; it was full of bones. He led me back and forth among them, and I saw a great many bones on the floor of the valley, bones that were very dry. He asked me, "Son of man, can these bones live?" I said, "Sovereign Lord, you alone know." Then he said to me, "Prophesy to these bones and say to them, 'Dry bones, hear the word of the Lord! This is what the Sovereign Lord says to these bones: I will make breath enter you, and you will come to life. I will attach tendons to you and make flesh come upon you and cover you with skin; I will put breath in you, and you will come to life. Then you will know that I am the Lord.' " So I prophesied as I was commanded. And as I was prophesying, there was a noise, a rattling sound, and the bones came together, bone to bone. I looked, and tendons and flesh appeared on them and skin covered them, but there was no breath in them. Then he said to me, "Prophesy to the breath; prophesy, son of man, and say to it, 'This is what the Sovereign Lord says: Come, breath, from the four winds and breathe into these slain, that they may live.' " So I prophesied as he commanded me, and breath entered them; they came to life and stood up on their feet—a vast army. Then he said to me: "Son of man, these bones are the people of Israel. They say, 'Our bones are dried up and our hope is gone; we are cut off.'

Then you, my people, will know that I am the Lord, when I open your graves and bring you up from them. I will put my Spirit in you and you will live, and I will settle you in your own land. Then you will know that I the Lord have spoken, and I have done it, declares the Lord.' ""

What we see is Ezekiel being captivated by the spirit to see a very detailed image. Throughout the book of Ezekiel we see him being led by the spirit in dreams or open visions. He is driven to speak whatever he has seen. When the Roeh has seen or envisioned, expect the Roeh to go into prophetic drama. The Roeh prophet will display a depth of the dramatic to get his or her point across. When the dramatic presentation has taken place the Roeh spirit will be settled as what they saw in the spirit realm has now been completed in the earth. As you can see the Roeh prophet is much different than that of the Nabi prophet. Although they both are prophets with access to the spirit realm, they differ from each other.

The Chozeh

The Chozeh prophet is described as "to see" or "to perceive". It's also used to reference a musician, a counselor, or an advisor to a king. The key phrase we'll explore to define the Chozeh and its function as a prophet is, "to perceive" which means, to recognize, discern, envision or understand, to distinguish, or to identify. How the Chozeh prophet can prophetically see is through natural things and events. Things in the natural realm or events triggers the prophet's sight and causes the prophet to see that which is going on in the spirit. This is not the only thing that causes the prophet to see, but it is the very core and foundation in which causes the prophet to understand what is going on in the spirit. The prophet Jeremiah exemplifies the foundation of the Chozeh prophet. In Jeremiah 1:11-13 we see the imagery of how the prophet looks and function. It reads:
"The word of the Lord came to me: What do you see, Jeremiah?" I see the branch of an almond tree," I replied. The Lord said to me, "You have seen correctly, for I am watching to see that my word is fulfilled." The word of the Lord came to me again: "What do you see?" I see a boiling pot, tilting away from the north.." (Jeremiah 1:11-13)

We see that Jeremiah can understand the prophetic word of what is naturally seen on the earth. It is through the sight of the Almond tree and the boiling pot that Jeremiah can see disaster coming to the land. In the book of Act 21:10 the prophet Agabus from Judea took Paul's belt and saw Paul being bound in Jerusalem and handed over to the Gentiles. What we see through all of this is the Chozeh prophet's ability to understand the coming of things by that which is natural. This is one of the abilities of the Chozeh prophet. The next image we see of the Chozeh prophet is the musical gift. In the book of 2 Samuel 23:1-2 we read of the Prophet David, whom the Lord is to speak prophetic oracles through music. It reads:

"The oracle of David's son Jesse, the oracle of the man exalted by the Most High, the man anointed by the God of Jacob, Israel's singer of songs. The Spirit of the Lord spoke through me; his word was on my tongue." 2 Samuel 23:1-2

The prophet David could release prophetic oracle through his musicianship. He was skilled in doing prophetic warfare through his musical oracles, bringing deliverance to Israel and Judah. But the most revealed is the identity of the Chozeh prophet through the life of David is his ability to release a song of deliverance to free the mind of King Saul.

"Whenever the spirit from God came upon Saul, David would take his harp and play. Then relief would come to Saul; he would feel better, and the evil spirit would leave him." (1Samuel 16:23)

The Chozeh prophet musicianship helps the prophet move in the realm of the spirit for deliverance and healing. When the prophet is in prophetic worship the prophet's ability to release a sound in the airwaves causes the systematic attacks of the enemy to be halted and the releasing of the power of healing takes place in the body, soul and spirit. This ability of the Chozeh prophet helps us to see the importance of the prophet understanding his or her gifts in music and the importance of them being educated in the tactics and strategies of warfare.

The third and final ability of the Chozeh prophet is his or her ability to give counsel and advice. The Lord has given the Chozeh prophet the wisdom to help leaders maneuver through the trials of leadership and the warfare of the enemy. We see this example through the life of Nathan the prophet as he counsels King David through his failure with Bathsheba.

"The Lord sent Nathan to David. When he came to him, he said, "There were two men in a certain town, one rich and the other poor. The rich man had a very large number of

sheep and cattle, but the poor man had nothing except one little ewe lamb he had bought. He raised it, and it grew up with him and his children. It shared his food, drank from his cup and even slept in his arms. It was like a daughter to him. "Now a traveler came to the rich man, but the rich man refrained from taking one of his own sheep or cattle to prepare a meal for the traveler who had come to him. Instead, he took the ewe lamb that belonged to the poor man and prepared it for the one who had come to him." David burned with anger against the man and said to Nathan, "As surely as the Lord lives, the man who did this must die! He must pay for that lamb four times over, because he did such a thing and had no pity." Then Nathan said to David, "You are the man! This is what the Lord, the God of Israel, says: 'I anointed you king over Israel, and I delivered you from the hand of Saul. I gave your master's house to you, and your master's wives into your arms. I gave you all Israel and Judah. And if all this had been too little, I would have given you even more. Why did you despise the word of the Lord by doing what is evil in his eyes? You struck down Uriah the Hittite with the sword and took his wife to be your own. You killed him with the sword of the Ammonites. Now, therefore, the sword will never depart from your house, because you despised me and took the wife of Uriah the Hittite to be your own."
(2 Samuel 12:1-10 NIV)

Nathan's example shows us how the Chozeh prophet has the ability to move among the leadership. His sensitivity to the leadership of the King and how to deal with the king shows us how critical the Chozeh prophet must possess the wisdom of the heart of God. David's failures need the right counsel and advice as to when failure or direction is needed among the leadership; the Lord prepares the Chozeh prophet to handle it.

The Ish'Elohim

The Ish'Elohim is the most unique prophet among the four and the most covet. This prophet was the very force of the Lord's hand. The Ish'Elohim is defined by the Hebrews as diviners, man of God, Holy Man, Possess by God, a Miracle worker, Angel of God and Man of Spirit. These seven identities describe a prophet meant to create wreckage against the kingdom of darkness. This Ish'Elohim represents the Image of God. Its first purpose is to establish and to protect the very image and glory of the Lord. When we look at the Ish'Elohim as a diviner we speak of the prophet's responsibility to bear the very Image of Yahweh, establish the Image of the Lord and protect it. We see that in the life of Elijah as he goes went against the prophets of Baal. Elijah's assignment is to dispose of and image created by the prophets of Baal. In order to this, Elijah must go to war.

"Then Elijah said to them, "I am the only one of the Lord's prophets left, but Baal has four hundred and fifty prophets. Get two bulls for us. Let Baal's prophets choose one for themselves, and let them cut it into pieces and put it on the wood but not set fire to it. I will prepare the other bull and put it on the wood but not set fire to it. Then you call on the name of your god, and I will call on the name of the Lord. The god who answers by fire—he is God." Then all the people said, "What you say is good." Elijah said to the prophets of Baal, "Choose one of the bulls and prepare it first, since there are so many of you. Call on the name of your god, but do not light the fire." So they took the bull given them and prepared it. Then they called on the name of Baal from morning till noon. "Baal, answer us!" They shouted. But there was no response; no one answered. And they danced around the altar they had made. At noon Elijah began to taunt them. "Shout louder!" He said. "Surely he is a god! Perhaps he is deep in thought, or busy, or traveling. Maybe he is sleeping and must be awakened." So they shouted louder and slashed themselves with swords and

spears, as was their custom, until their blood flowed. Midday passed, and they continued their frantic prophesying until the time for the evening sacrifice. But there was no response, no one answered, no one paid attention. Then Elijah said to all the people, "Come here to me." They came to him, and he repaired the altar of the Lord, which had been torn down. Elijah took twelve stones, one for each of the tribes descended from Jacob, to whom the word of the Lord had come, saying, "Your name shall be Israel." With the stones he built an altar in the name of the Lord, and he dug a trench around it large enough to hold two seahs of seed. He arranged the wood, cut the bull into pieces and laid it on the wood. Then he said to them, "Fill four large jars with water and pour it on the offering and on the wood." "Do it again," he said, and they did it again. "Do it a third time," he ordered, and they did it the third time. The water ran down around the altar and even filled the trench. At the time of sacrifice, the prophet Elijah stepped forward and prayed: " Lord, the God of Abraham, Isaac and Israel, let it be known today that you are God in Israel and that I am your servant and have done all these things at your command. Answer me, Lord, answer me, so these people will know that you, Lord, are God, and that you are turning their hearts back again." Then the fire of the Lord fell and burned up the sacrifice, the wood, the stones and the soil, and also licked up the water in the trench. When all the people saw this, they fell prostrate and cried, "The Lord —he is God! The Lord —he is God!" (1 Kings 18:22-39 NIV)

Baal is described by the Hebrew as, master and Lord. Ethbaal the father of Jezebel sought to establish Baalism in the life and culture of Israel. The purpose for such was to shift the identity of Yahweh, and establish the image of Baal. The prophets of Baal purpose was to make sure that Baals image was established to take the place of Yahweh. When Elijah walks in his divine purpose as the Ish'Elohim (The Diviner), it is to ensure that the Image of Yahweh is not lost in Israel. The Hebrew name for this is, "Eliayahu" which means My God is

Yahweh. He must protect the sacredness of Yahweh image and the establishment of the covenant that represents it. For Elijah to do such a thing he must go to war with the prophets of Baal. We see this first about Ish'Elohim purpose in the earth. They are proctors of the image and they must cherish that responsibility.

The Ish' Elohim as a Man of God represents the deep and in tune relationship they have with Yahweh. The Ish'Elohim life is consumed by prayer and their action is such. This does not mean the other prophet's don't live in prayer, but the Ish'Elohim life is seen in prayer. Moses In Deuteronomy 33:1 is the first in biblical history to be called Man of God. In The book of Exodus we see throughout Moses' relationship with Yahweh so much so that when Miriam spoke against Moses in Numbers 12:4-8 the Lord gets angry and calls them all to the tent of meeting to discuss the matter. When they came into the tent of meeting the Lord defined the difference between HIS relationship with Moses and HIS relationship with Miriam. Separating the two that she may understand that Moses reflected who he was as Yahweh.

"At once the Lord said to Moses, Aaron and Miriam, "Come out to the tent of meeting, all three of you." So the three of them went out. Then the Lord came down in a pillar of cloud; he stood at the entrance to the tent and summoned Aaron and Miriam. When the two of them stepped forward, he said, "Listen to my words: "When there is a prophet among you, I, the Lord, reveal myself to them in visions, I speak to them in dreams. But this is not true of my servant Moses; he is faithful in all my house. With him I speak face to face, clearly and not in riddles; he sees the form of the Lord. Why then were you not afraid to speak against my servant Moses?" (Numbers 12:4-8 NIV)

This is what the Ish' Elohim represents as the Man of God. They represent His Glory, His Image, His power. The Ish'Elohim becomes the reflections of what he sees. Yahweh actually becomes the embodiment of the things he learns prior to becoming Yahweh.

"Then the Lord said to him, "What is that in your hand?" "A staff," he replied. The Lord said, "Throw it on the ground." Moses threw it on the ground and it became a snake, and he ran from it. Then the Lord said to him, "Reach out your hand and take it by the tail." So Moses reached out and took hold of the snake and it turned back into a staff in his hand. "This," said the Lord, "is so that they may believe that the Lord, the God of their fathers—the God of Abraham, the God of Isaac and the God of Jacob—has appeared to you." Then the Lord said, "Put your hand inside your cloak." So Moses put his hand into his cloak, and when he took it out, the skin was leprous —it had become as white as snow. "Now put it back into your cloak," he said. So Moses put his hand back into his cloak, and when he took it out, it was restored, like the rest of his flesh. Exodus 4:2-7 NIV

The Ish'Elohim as a holy man signifies him being set apart for the work and lifestyle in which he was called. His consecration is very important because it speaks of the source of his power and authority. As a holy man the Ish'Elohim can prophetically speak because of his consecration. It allows him to hear therefore act on behalf of the kingdom. Moses the prophet is considered to be such a man. In Exodus 33:11-17 we read God's blue print of such a man:

"So the LORD spoke to Moses face to face, as a man speaks to his friend. And he would return to the camp, but his servant Joshua the son of Nun, a young man, did not depart from the tabernacle. Then Moses said to the LORD, "See, You say to me, 'Bring up this people.' But You have not let me know whom You will send with me. Yet You have said, 'I know you by name, and you have also found grace in My sight.' Now therefore, I pray, if I have found grace in Your sight, show me now Your way, that I may know You and that

I may find grace in Your sight. And consider that this nation is Your people." And He said, "My Presence will go with you, and I will give you rest." Then he said to Him, "If Your Presence does not go with us, do not bring us up from here. For how then will it be known that Your people and I have found grace in Your sight, except You go with us? So we shall be separate, Your people and I, from all the people who are upon the face of the earth." So the LORD said to Moses, "I will also do this thing that you have spoken; for you have found grace in My sight, and I know you by name." (Exodus 33:11-17 NKJV)

The Ish'Elohim possessed by God, represents power and authority of the Ish'Elohim. Ish'Elohim is filled with the power to perform the miraculous which includes the authority to shut up the heavens. Ish'Elohim's ability to do such a work stems from them being captivated by God and empowered by His presence. With such

a possession the Ish'Elohim can do things like no other prophet. Elijah was given the speed to run faster than Ahab after he sent Ahab ahead of him before the rain began and then prayed for the rain to come, struggle to produce the rain and then got the rain to come after his presentence in prayer. He then ran and beat Ahab before he arrived at his destination. Another example is that of Jesus' ability to walk on water, turn water into wine and turning two fish and five loaves of bread into an abundant meal. What we see with the possession of the Ish'Elohim is God purpose to deal with those created things, which have fallen out of alignment or have been damaged by the forces of darkness to be restored, recreated or brought back in order. This is the very reason the Ish'Elohim is called 'possessed of God'. The Ish'Elohim as the Miracle worker points to the prophet's ability to deal with those things, which are dead; meaning, an entity in creation was interrupted and is no longer on divine schedule. The Ish'Elohim comes to make sure that such an act in the earth is interrupted; what God has created and chosen stays on its divine course to fulfill its divine agenda. When direction is lost through death, the Ish'Elohim as the miracle workers assures the restoration of life and direction to those that have lost their way. We see this with the Prophet Elisha in 2 Kings 4:17-37

"But the woman conceived, and bore a son when the appointed time had come, of which Elisha had told her. And the child grew. Now it happened one day that he went out to his father, to the reapers. And he said to his father, "My head, my head!" So he said to a servant, "Carry him to his mother." When he had taken him, and brought him to his mother, he sat on her knees till noon, and then died. And she went up and laid him on the bed of the man of God, shut the door upon him, and went out. Then she called to her husband, and said, "Please send me one of the young men and one of the donkeys, that I may run to the man of God and come back." So he said, "Why are you going to him today? It is neither the New Moon nor the Sabbath." And she said, " It is well." Then she saddled a donkey, and said to her servant, "Drive, and go forward; do not slacken the pace for me unless I tell you." And so she departed, and went to the man of God at Mount Carmel. So it was, when the man of God saw her afar off, that he said to his servant Gehazi, "Look, the Shunammite woman! Please run now to meet her, and say to her, ' Is it well with you? Is it well with your husband? Is it well with the child?' " And she answered, "It is well." Now when she came to the man of God at the hill, she caught him by the feet, but Gehazi came near to push her away. But the man of God said, "Let her alone; for her soul is in deep distress, and the LORD has hidden it from me, and has not told me." So she said, "Did I ask a son of my lord? Did I not say, 'Do not deceive me'?" Then he said to Gehazi, "Get yourself ready, and take my staff in your hand, and be on your way. If you meet anyone, do not greet him; and if anyone greets you, do not answer him; but lay my staff on the face of the child." And the mother of the child said, "As the LORD lives, and as your soul lives, I will not leave you." So

he arose and followed her. Now Gehazi went on ahead of them, and laid the staff on the face of the child; but there was neither voice nor hearing. Therefore, he went back to meet him, and told him, saying, "The child has not awakened." When Elisha came into the house, there was the child, lying dead on his bed. He went in therefore, shut the door behind the two of them, and prayed to the LORD. And he went up and lay on the child, and put his mouth on his mouth, his eyes on his eyes, and his hands on his hands; and he stretched himself out on the child, and the flesh of the child became warm. He returned and walked back and forth in the house, and again went up, and stretched himself out on him; then the child sneezed seven times, and the child opened his eyes. And he called Gehazi, and said, "Call this Shunammite woman." So he called her. And when she came in to him, he said, "Pick up your son." So she went in, fell at his feet, and bowed to the ground; then she picked up her son and went out." (II Kings 4:17-37 NKJV)

The Ish'Elohim as the Angel of God speaks to his or her mission on the earth. Angels are submitted to the strict obedience of the Lord. The angel's responsibility is to focus on one thing and one thing only - the assignment and mission of the Lord in which they were called to embark upon. So it is with the Ish'Elohim of the Lord. Their imagery as the Angel of God speaks to their angelic obedience to the Lord and the things of the spirit. They are strict for fulfilling the mission of the Lord. They seek to bring the Lord glory in their obedience. Fulfilling every mandate given to them. The Prophet Elisha shows us this in 2 Kings 9:1-4

"The prophet Elisha summoned a man from the company of the prophets and said to him, "Tuck your cloak into your belt, take this flask of olive oil with you and go to Ramoth Gilead. When you get there, look for Jehu son of Jehoshaphat, the son of Nimshi. Go to him, get him away from his companions and take him into an inner room. Then take the flask and pour the oil on his head and declare, 'This is what the Lord

says: I anoint you king over Israel.' Then open the door and run; don't delay!" So the young prophet went to Ramoth Gilead." (2 Kings 9:1-4)

The Man of the Spirit speaks of the Ish'Elohim humanity, yet his divinity as a prophet of the Lord. The power of the spirit in which the Ish'Elohim possess in his or her humanity speaks to the prophet's weakness and its dependence on the power of the spirit to overcome, that which is within, and that which is out. The Imagery here of the Ish'Elohim shows us the power that the prophets possess to move beyond carnal things, or to conquer them as it relates to the flesh. The Ish'Elohim as a Man of the Spirit details him or her as a man or woman of warfare speaking of the prophet's ability to deal with the carnal realm according to the spirit. We see this example with Jesus in the wilderness in Luke 11:1-13

"Jesus, full of the Holy Spirit, left the Jordan and was led by the Spirit into the wilderness, where for forty days he was tempted by the devil. He ate nothing during those days, and at the end of them he was hungry. The devil said to him, "If you are the Son of God, tell this stone to become bread." Jesus answered, "It is written: 'Man shall not live on bread alone.' " The devil led him up to a high place and showed him in an instant all the kingdoms of the world. And he said to him, "I will give you all their authority and splendor; it has been given to me, and I can give it to anyone I want to. If you worship me, it will all be yours." Jesus answered, "It is written: 'Worship the Lord your God and serve him only.' " The devil led him to Jerusalem and had him stand on the highest point of the temple. "If you are the Son of God," he said, "throw yourself down from here. For it is written: "He will command his angels concerning you to guard you carefully; they will lift you up in their hands, so that you will not strike your foot against a stone.' " Jesus answered, "It is said: 'Do not put the Lord your God to the test.' " When the devil had finished all this tempting, he left him until an opportune time."

(Luke 11:1-13, NIV)

The four prophets mentioned here are thoroughly explained so you may clearly understand which prophet you are destined to be. Knowing your prophetic destiny, enables you to define your direction and placement in the body of Christ - *(The three placements will be explained in the next chapter)*. But understand that most of the prophetic chaos in today's church is the budding of young prophets and the Prophets of Old not identifying their true prophetic makeup. Because of this, the prophets have become more zealous to prophesy than to sit in the proper training to help them understand such an identity. What I have explained in this chapter are the four prophets. They were identified those four prophets and explain or define their function in the prophetic office. It is up to you, the reader, the student and the prophet to allow the above information in these chapters to challenge you to look within and figure out your identity as the prophet of the Lord. You can only do this if you'll face the reality of what the prophetic office looks like among these four prophets.

THE PLACEMENT

CHAPTER FIVE

The Placement

As we enter the prophetic office understand that every prophet after going through the proper training and figuring out what prophet they are must be placed somewhere. We call this prophetic placement. The Bible describes three major places where the Hebrew prophets were assigned. These three placements were the center of prophetic revelation, actions and moments. The prophets assigned to these places were to bring clarity of the Lord's heart and to his people. These places were known as the Palace - place of political tension, the Temple - place of the Lord's court, and the Field - place of the world systems, lost souls, missed direction and broken places. These key places are among us today. As we look out today we see The Palace as our government, The Temple as today's church, and the Field as the place of world systems, broken places and people. As the prophet develops he or she will have to recognize which place the Lord is calling them. This understanding will help empower the prophet's mantle. My job in this book is to help you understand these places and how they play an important role of the prophet's destiny.

The chaos among today's prophets stem from the majority of them not understanding their placement in the earth. Prophets of today have gone wherever they wanted with no regard to discipline and restriction. They have lost sight of the boundaries of the prophetic office and gone off of a charismatic zeal which pushes them into a place of rebellion without them even knowing it. This is because many prophets of old did not teach today's prophets about placement. Inside of placement there is boundaries, discipline, restrictions and protocol. No prophet can take it upon himself or herself to choose their placement. This duty is Yahweh, and Yahweh alone. The placement is given to assure that the prophetic utterance of Yahweh is established and the place in which he has assigned the prophet and to make sure, that place is flourishing under the mantle of that prophet. Meaning, there is a grace and anointing given to that prophet to make sure that prosperity takes place where that prophet has been appointed. That leads us to define the word placement and what does that mean for the prophets of the 21st century.

The word placement is defined as the action of putting someone or something in a particular place. The Greek meaning defines it as, filling a position or arrangement. The Bible shows us such a meaning when Elijah flees to mountain Horeb. Here the Lord's speak to Elijah about his place being fulfilled by Elisha. It reads:

"The Lord said to him, "Go back the way you came, and go to the Desert of Damascus. When you get there, anoint Hazael king over Aram. Also, anoint Jehu son of Nimshi king over Israel, and anoint Elisha son of Shaphat from Abel Meholah to succeed you as prophet." (1 Kings 19:15-16)

The passage of scripture shows us there was a vacancy opening up regarding the mantle of Elijah, and that is the key statement right there. That the placement was regarding the mantle of Elijah that had to be carried on. Still work was done in the region or territory in which Elijah was assigned and the Lord had found a replacement for him. Elisha responsibility was to fulfill the assignment given to Elijah. It was his mandate and appointment into the region and territory which Elijah was assigned. Elisha knew that his placement had everything to do with the mantle in which he picked up. It states in 2Kings 2:11-15

"As they were walking along and talking together, suddenly a chariot of fire and horses of fire appeared and separated the two of them, and Elijah went up to heaven in a whirlwind. Elisha saw this and cried out, "My father! My father! The chariots and horsemen of Israel!" And Elisha saw him no more. Then he took hold of his garment and tore it in two. Elisha then picked up Elijah's cloak that had fallen from him and went back and stood on the bank of the Jordan. He took the cloak that had fallen from Elijah and struck the water with it. "Where now is the Lord, the God of Elijah?" He asked. When he struck the water, it divided to the right and to the left, and he crossed over. The company of the prophets from Jericho, who were watching, said, "The spirit of Elijah is resting on Elisha." And they went to meet him and bowed to the ground before him." (2 Kings 2:11-15 NIV)

Now as we read the above statement and scripture we can see that the Lord needs to place a prophet in the right placement for the sake of finishing the work of mantles he has given instruction. Most places the prophets have been assigned, were abandoned due to the imagery of the culture and how that culture demanded the prophet to represent it. The mantles of the Prophets of Old have been forsaken. Prophets of today have created their own mantles, built their own zeal, and develop and obtain their own purpose. No more does the prophetic utterance of old matter to today's young prophets. For the prosperity of such places have hinged on the very revelation of the prophetic mantle only to be silenced by the self-desire of a rebellious prophet. Only if we could understand the importance of placement of the prophet.

The three major placements in which the prophet is assigned to in the earth helps bring forth the Lord's influence and his dominion in the earth. Before I explain these three placements let me first go back and restate the opening points of this chapter. The placement in which every prophet has been called or embarks upon has everything to do with the prophetic mantles left behind in those regions or places. This mantle fulfills the assigned mandate given over that region or place. Understanding the importance of these three placements is vital to the success of the prophet's mantle.

The Palace (The Government)

"Now it came to pass, when the king was dwelling in his house, and the LORD had given him rest from all his enemies all around, that the king said to Nathan the prophet, "See now, I dwell in a house of cedar, but the ark of God dwells inside tent curtains." Then Nathan said to the king, "Go, do all that is in your heart, for the LORD is with you." But it happened that night, that the word of the LORD came to Nathan, saying, "Go and tell My servant David, 'Thus says the LORD: "Would you build a house for Me to dwell in?" (II Samuel 7:1-5 NKJV)

The King's Court was the place of decision and direction of the Hebrew people. Here in the King's court officials of the King's, counselor, wise men and others gather together to discuss the outcome of governmental affairs. Here in the King's Courts the political agenda, was born. Political fever causes those who sought justice to sometime fail in getting a favorable outcome. It also builds a reputation of low-balling the people for taxes, food, land and business. The Lord place a Prophet among the courts of his Kings. Forever king in the history of Israel and Judah a prophet was assigned to that King. That prophet would make sure, that King understood the direction of the Lord. We see this action when King David falls with Bathsheba, Uriah's wife:

"Then the LORD sent Nathan to David. And he came to him, and said to him: "There were two men in one city, one rich and the other poor. The rich man had exceedingly many more flocks and herds. But the poor man had nothing, except one little ewe lamb, which he had bought and

nourished; and it grew up together with him and with his children. It ate of his own food and drank from his own cup, and lay in his bosom; and it was like a daughter to him. And a traveler came to the rich man, who refused to take from his own flock and from his own herd, to prepare one for the wayfaring man who had come to him; but he took the poor man's lamb and prepared it for the man who had come to him." So David's anger was greatly aroused against the man, and he said to Nathan, "As the LORD lives, the man who has done this shall surely die! And he shall restore fourfold for the lamb, because he did this thing and because he had no pity." Then Nathan said to David, "You are the man! Thus says the LORD God of Israel: 'I anointed you king over Israel, and I delivered you from the hand of Saul. I gave you your master's house and your master's wives into your keeping, and gave you the house of Israel and Judah. And if that had been too little, I also would have given you much more! Why have you despised the commandment of the LORD, to do evil in His sight? You have killed Uriah the Hittite with the sword; you have taken his wife to be your wife, and have killed him with the sword of the people of Ammon. Now therefore, the sword shall never depart from your house, because you have despised Me, and have taken the wife of Uriah the Hittite to be your wife.' Thus says the LORD: 'Behold, I will raise up adversity against you from your own house; and I will take your wives before your eyes and give them to your neighbor, and he shall lie with your wives in the sight of this sun. For you did it secretly, but I will do this thing before all Israel, before the sun.' " So David said to Nathan, "I have sinned against the LORD." And Nathan said to David, "The LORD also has put away your sin; you shall not die. However, because by this deed you have given great occasion to the enemies of the LORD to blaspheme, the child also who is born to you shall surely die." Then Nathan departed to his house. And the LORD struck the child that Uriah's wife bore to David, and it became ill.
(II Samuel 12:1-15 NKJV)

As we look at the Palace prophet there are five things that the Palace Prophet will handle:

1. They help establish political leadership and its government.

The prophet Samuel helped to establish the Monarchy and government in Israel. He taught the people how to deal with political leadership and the order of government.

"Then Samuel took a flask of oil and poured it on his head, and kissed him and said: Is it not because the LORD has anointed you commander over His inheritance?"(I Samuel 10:1 NKJV)

""Then Samuel explained to the people the behavior of royalty, and wrote it in a book and laid it up before the LORD. And Samuel sent all the people away, every man to his house." (I Samuel 10:25 NKJV)

What you see with both scriptures is that Samuel established royal leadership and then taught the people how they should behave for leadership. The palace prophet must understand this is one of their responsibilities.
They will be guided in helping governments become established.

2. They deal with the behavior of political leadership.

"Now the word of the LORD came to Samuel, saying, "I greatly regret that I have set up Saul as king, for he has turned back from following Me, and has not performed My commandments." And it grieved Samuel, and he cried out to the LORD all night. So when Samuel rose early in the morning to meet Saul, it was told Samuel, saying, "Saul went to Carmel, and indeed, he set up a monument for himself; and he has gone on around, passed by, and gone down to Gilgal." Then Samuel went to Saul, and Saul said to him, "Blessed are you of the LORD! I have performed the commandment of the LORD." But Samuel said, "What then is this bleating of the sheep in my ears, and the lowing of the oxen which I hear?" And Saul said, "They have brought them from the Amalekites; for the people spared the best of the sheep and the oxen, to sacrifice to the LORD your God; and the rest we have utterly destroyed." Then Samuel said to Saul, "Be quiet! And I will tell you what the LORD said to me last night." And he said to him, "Speak on." So Samuel said, "When you were little in your own eyes, were you not head of the tribes of Israel? And did not the LORD anoint you king over Israel? Now the LORD sent you on a mission, and said, 'Go, and utterly destroy the sinners, the Amalekites, and fight against them until they are consumed.' Why then did you not obey the voice of the LORD? Why did you swoop down on the spoil, and do evil in the sight of the LORD?" And Saul said to Samuel, "But I have obeyed the voice of the LORD, and gone on the mission on which the LORD sent me, and brought back Agag king of Amalek; I have utterly destroyed the Amalekites. But the people took of the plunder, sheep and oxen, the best of the things which should have been utterly destroyed, to sacrifice to the LORD your God in Gilgal." So Samuel said: "Has the LORD, as great delight in burnt offerings and sacrifices, As in obeying the voice of the LORD? Behold, to obey is better than sacrifice, And to heed than the fat of rams. For rebellion is as the sin of witchcraft, And stubbornness is as iniquity and idolatry. Because you have rejected the word of the LORD, He also has rejected you from being king." (I Samuel 15:10-23 NKJV)

The prophet Samuel must deal with Saul, as he does not carry out the instructions of the Lord. Because of this disobedience Saul brought a season of chaos upon the Lord's people and caused a generational effect that would cause the seed of Agag to rise up and try to annihilate the Lord's people in the book of Esther. It is the job of the Palace prophet to deal with such behavior that would cost the Lord's people.

3. The palace prophet deals with the enemies that attack their nation.

"Come near, you nations, to hear; And heed, you people! Let the earth hear, and all that is in it, The world and all things that come forth from it. For the indignation of the LORD is against all nations, And His fury against all their armies; He has utterly destroyed them, He has given them over to the slaughter. Also, their slain shall be thrown out; Their stench shall rise from their corpses, And the mountains shall be melted with their blood. All the host of heaven shall be dissolved, And the heavens shall be rolled up like a scroll; All their host shall fall down As the leaf falls from the vine, And as fruit falling from a fig tree. "For My sword shall be bathed in heaven; Indeed, it shall come down on Edom, And for the people of My curse, for judgment. The sword of the LORD is filled with blood, It is made overflowing with fatness, With the blood of lambs and goats, With the fat of the kidneys of rams. For the LORD has a sacrifice in Bozrah, And a great slaughter in the land of Edom. The wild oxen shall come down with them, And the young bulls with the mighty bulls; Their land shall be soaked with blood, And their dust saturated with fatness." For it is the day of the LORD's vengeance, The year of recompense for the cause of Zion." (Isaiah 34:1-8 NKJV)

'The palace prophet must uphold the banner of righteousness against the nations that would try to remove the Lord's hand of favor off that nation in which the prophet is prophetically called to give utterance. This thought also applies to the Prophet's responsibility to make sure that the nation it is called to, understand the Lord's heart for His people Israel. The palace prophet must remind those that would attempt to assassinate those the Lord has favored, that God's protection is strong and those that would try to oppose the hand of the Lord will be dispensed.

4. The Prophet must make sure that the right political leader takes the seat of honor.

"And King David said, "Call to me Zadok the priest, Nathan the prophet, and Benaiah the son of Jehoiada." So they came before the king. The king also said to them, "Take with you the servants of your lord, and have Solomon my son ride on my own mule, and take him down to Gihon. There let Zadok the priest and Nathan the prophet anoint him king over Israel; and blow the horn, and say, ' Long live King Solomon!' Then you shall come up after him, and he shall come and sit on my throne, and he shall be king in my place. For I have appointed him to be ruler over Israel and Judah."(I Kings 1:32-35 NKJV)

The Palace prophet must make sure those who are rising up in leadership are the set voice that the Lord has in place to lead the nation. The Prophet should have his or her ear to the heart of the Lord. Nathan the prophet when he saw that the seat of honor was taken illegally, he moved under prophetic wisdom to make sure that the King, the Lord has chosen would be the one to rise in power. He stated:

"So Nathan spoke to Bathsheba the mother of Solomon, saying, "Have you not heard that Adonijah the son of Haggith has become king, and David our lord does not know it? Come, please, let me now give you advice, that you may save your own life and the life of your son Solomon. Go immediately to King David and say to him, 'Did you not, my lord, O king, swear to your maidservant, saying, "Assuredly your son Solomon shall reign after me, and he shall sit on my throne"? Why then has Adonijah become king?' Then, while you are still talking there with the king, I also will come in after you and confirm your words." (I Kings 1:11-14 NKJV)

5. The Palace Prophet must be able to reveal the writing on the wall.

"Then Daniel was brought in before the king. The king spoke, and said to Daniel, " Are you that Daniel who is one of the captives from Judah, whom my father the king brought from Judah? I have heard of you, that the Spirit of God is in you, and that light and understanding and excellent wisdom are found in you. Now the wise men, the astrologers, have been brought in before me, that they should read this writing, and make known to me its interpretation, but they could not give the interpretation of the thing. And I have heard of you, that you can give interpretations and explain enigmas. Now if you can read the writing and make known to me its interpretation, you shall be clothed with purple and have a chain of gold around your neck, and shall be the third ruler in the kingdom." (Daniel 5:13-16 NKJV)

The Palace prophet must be able to understand that the weight of trouble will come to every leadership, but they must be ready to explain the very thing that troubles that leader in private. The weight of leadership is burdensome, but the Lord put a prophet in the palace to make sure that he reveals to that leader the writings on the wall.

These five responsibilities I have explained to you will help the palace prophet understand the assignment and mission of their office. These points will bring focus to the palace prophet's mission bringing clarity and understanding to those that are called to be in the palace.

The Temple (The Church)

"Now there was one, Anna, a prophetess, the daughter of Phanuel, of the tribe of Asher. She was of a great age, and had lived with a husband seven years from her virginity; and this woman was a widow of about eighty-four years, who did not depart from the temple, but served God with fastings and prayers night and day." (Luke 2:36-37 NKJV)

The Temple prophet comes to define the responsibility of the church and to make sure that it is pushed into its divine purpose. The prophet establishment in the temple helps the Lord's people to understand their responsibility to the church. There are six points the temple prophet must understand:

1. The temple prophet (Church Prophet) must protect the Covenant of the Church.

"And Moses turned, and went down from the mountain, and the two tablets of the Testimony were in his hand. The tablets were written on both sides; on the one side and on the other they were written. Now the tablets were the work of God, and the writing was the writing of God engraved on the tablets. And when Joshua heard the noise of the people as they shouted, he said to Moses, " There is a noise of war in the camp." But he said: " It is not the noise of the shout of victory, Nor the noise of the cry of defeat, But the sound of singing I hear." So it was, as soon as he came near the camp, that he saw the calf and the dancing. So Moses' anger became hot, and he cast the tablets out of his hands and broke them at the foot of the mountain."(Exodus 32:15-19 NKJV)

"And the LORD said to Moses, "Cut two tablets of stone like the first ones, and I will write on these tablets the words that were on the first tablets which you broke. So be ready in the morning, and come up in the morning to Mount Sinai, and present yourself to Me there on the top of the mountain. And no man shall come up with you, and let no man be seen throughout all the mountain; let neither flocks nor herds feed before that mountain." So he cut two tablets of stone like the first ones. Then Moses rose early in the morning and went up Mount Sinai, as the LORD had commanded him; and he took in his hand the two tablets of stone. Now the LORD descended in the cloud and stood with him there, and proclaimed the name of the LORD. And the LORD passed

before him and proclaimed, "The LORD, the LORD God, merciful and gracious, long-suffering, and abounding in goodness and truth, keeping mercy for thousands, forgiving iniquity and transgression and sin, by no means clearing the guilty, visiting the iniquity of the fathers upon the children and the children's children to the third and the fourth generation." So Moses made haste and bowed his head toward the earth, and worshiped. Then he said, "If now I have found grace in Your sight, O Lord, let my Lord, I pray, go among us, even though we are a stiff-necked people; and pardon our iniquity and our sin, and take us as Your inheritance." And He said: "Behold, I make a covenant. Before all your people I will do marvels, such as have not been done in all the earth, nor in any nation; and all the people among whom you are shall see the work of the LORD. For it is an awesome thing that I will do with you."
(Exodus 34:1-10 NKJV)

The temple prophet carries the burden of making sure that the covenant in which the church is under is not broken in any way. The covenant in which the church is under symbolize the relationship, assignment and mission in which the church has been established. The prophet helps gives voice to that covenant, helping the church stay the course and making sure that the covenant is not broken. If the covenant is broken, the temple prophet must then prophetically engage to seek why the covenant has been broken and then make sure the covenant is back intact. The temple prophet does this by prophetic wisdom, understanding that the Pastor is the leader of the house. He or she comes alongside the pastor to see what has taken place. If the pastor causes such error, then the prophet will issue a rebuke to the pastor and then seek the Lord for the direction of the church. No prophet may remove a pastor, only the Lord does. If the error is severe enough, the Lord will use those he put in place at that church to remove the pastor. The focus for such a prophet is to protect the covenant and release the word of the Lord. Remember

Moses did not remove Aaron from his place as high priest, but the Lord took it upon himself to remove him at the right time.

2. The Temple Prophet (Church Prophet) is responsible for the scariness of the house.

"Then the LORD spoke to Moses, saying: "On the first day of the first month you shall set up the tabernacle of the tent of meeting. You shall put in it the ark of the Testimony, and partition off the ark with the veil. You shall bring in the table and arrange the things that are to be set in order on it; and you shall bring in the lampstand and light its lamps. You shall also set the altar of gold for the incense before the ark of the Testimony, and put up the screen for the door of the tabernacle. Then you shall set the altar of the burnt offering before the door of the tabernacle of the tent of meeting. And you shall set the laver between the tabernacle of meeting and the altar, and put water in it. You shall set up the court all around, and hang up the screen at the court gate. "And you shall take the anointing oil, and anoint the tabernacle and all that is in it; and you shall hallow it and all its utensils, and it shall be holy. You shall anoint the altar of the burnt offering and all its utensils, and consecrate the altar. The altar shall be most holy. And you shall anoint the laver and its base, and consecrate it. "Then you shall bring Aaron and his sons to the door of the tabernacle of meeting and wash them with water. You shall put the holy garments on Aaron, and anoint him, and consecrate him, that he may minister to Me as priest. And you shall bring his sons, and clothe them with tunics. You shall anoint them, as you anointed their father, that they may minister to Me as priests; for their anointing shall surely be an everlasting priesthood throughout their generations." Thus Moses did; according to all that the LORD had commanded him, so he did. And it came to pass in the first month of the second year, on the first day of the month that the tabernacle was raised up. So Moses raised up the tabernacle, fastened its sockets, set up

its boards, put in its bars, and raised up its pillars. And he spread out the tent over the tabernacle and put the covering of the tent on top of it, as the LORD had commanded Moses. He took the Testimony and put it into the ark, inserted the poles through the rings of the ark, and put the mercy seat on top of the ark. And he brought the ark into the tabernacle, hung up the veil of the covering, and partitioned off the ark of the Testimony, as the LORD had commanded Moses. He put the table in the tabernacle of meeting, on the north side of the tabernacle, outside the veil; and he set the bread in order upon it before the LORD, as the LORD had commanded Moses. He put the lampstand in the tabernacle of meeting, across from the table, on the south side of the tabernacle; and he lit the lamps before the LORD, as the LORD had commanded Moses. He put the gold altar in the tabernacle of meeting in front of the veil; and he burned sweet incense on it, as the LORD had commanded Moses. He hung up the screen at the door of the tabernacle. And he put the altar of burnt offering before the door of the tabernacle of the tent of meeting, and offered upon it the burnt offering and the grain offering, as the LORD had commanded Moses. He set the laver between the tabernacle of meeting and the altar, and put water there for washing; and Moses, Aaron, and his sons would wash their hands and their feet with water from it. Whenever they went into the tabernacle of meeting, and when they came near the altar, they washed, as the LORD had commanded Moses. And he raised up the court all around the tabernacle and the altar, and hung up the screen of the court gate. So Moses finished the work." Exodus 40:1-33 NKJV

What I desire for you to see at this section is Moses' responsibility in handling the sacred things inside the house of the Lord. The prophet's heart is to make sure those things, which are established by God, is protected and held up. The oil, the presence of the Lord, and the consecration of his people are all the responsibility of the temple prophet. If the temple prophet fails at protecting the house sacredness, then the seed of corruption will bloom and the Lord will leave the house.

3. The temple prophet (Church Prophet) is responsible for covering the house in prayer.

"Now there was one, Anna, a prophetess, the daughter of Phanuel, of the tribe of Asher. She was of a great age, and had lived with a husband seven years from her virginity; and this woman was a widow of about eighty-four years, who did not depart from the temple, but served God with fastings and prayers night and day." (Luke 2:36-37 NKJV)

The temple prophet is saturated with the ministry of intercession inside the house of the Lord. Their focus is to make sure that prayer is being established in the house so the revelation of the heart of God is released in the Temple. The intercession released inside the house keeps the altar of fire burning and the presence of the Holy Spirit flows inside the house of the Lord. Because of this, those that enter the temple will experience the redemption of our Christ.

4. The temple prophet (Church Prophet) makes sure that the Church is evolving.

"Having been built on the foundation of the apostles and prophets, Jesus Christ Himself being the chief corner stone, in whom the whole building, being fitted together, grows into a holy temple in the Lord," (Ephesians 2:20-21 NKJV)

The church must evolve into who she was created to be. She cannot do that if she remains stagnant. It is the responsibility of the temple prophet to make sure that she does not get stagnant, but continues to evolve into whom she is. This will be one of the greatest challenges for the temple prophet as he/she must deal with the personalities and spirits that will try to mask itself and penetrate the very existence of the Body of Christ. She is calling for development and the temple prophet must make sure she does just that.

5. The temple Prophet (Church Prophet) is responsible for the edifying of the Church.

"And He Himself gave some to be apostles, some prophets, some evangelists, and some pastors and teachers, for the equipping of the saints for the work of ministry, for the edifying of the body of Christ," (Ephesians 4:11-12 NKJV)

The Lord uses the temple prophet to take the church to the next level. They become responsible for assisting everyone in the fivefold ministry by teaching, developing, and to restructure those who come into the church. The temple prophet must edify the church to the place chosen by the Lord. The Greek word for edify is "oikodomeo". It means to build a house or to build someone up helping them to stand or be strong. It is the prophet's responsibility that the house of the Lord is built up but it is also important that he or she strengthens those who enter into the house of the Lord. If the prophet fails to do this, the progression of the church becomes is hindered and the people whom entered into the church becomes vulnerable at the hand of the enemy.

6. The temple prophet (Church Prophet) must unlock the mystery of Christ concerning the church.

"He made known to me the mystery (as I have briefly written already, by which, when you read, you may understand my knowledge in the mystery of Christ), which in other ages was not made known to the sons of men, as it has now been revealed by the Spirit to His holy apostles and prophets:" (Ephesians 3:3-5 NKJV)

From the beginning of time the Lord has released mysteries concerning the church. The temple prophet must be in place to unlock these mysteries so those who come into the church may know what the Lord has prepared for them since the beginning of time. It is the temple prophet's responsibility to unlock those mysteries. If the prophet is absent from the temple, then the mysteries that were ordained to be unlocked in that dispensation is hindered, and those inside the church cannot experience the things in which God has prepared for them since the foundation of the world.

The six points above are important for the temple prophet to understand. Without them the church cannot understand her purpose, nor can she reach her destiny. It is vital that the temple prophet understand that they must understand these things before they are placed in the temple because they are the foundation for their placement.

The Field (The World)

"And you, child, will be called the prophet of the Highest; For you will go before the face of the Lord to prepare His ways, To give knowledge of salvation to His people By the remission of their sins, Through the tender mercy of our God, With which the Dayspring from on high has visited us; To give light to those who sit in darkness and the shadow of death, To guide our feet into the way of peace." So the child grew and became strong in spirit, and was in the deserts till the day of his manifestation to Israel." (Luke 1:76-80 NKJV)

The Field Prophet arises out of the wilderness to engage the demonic influence that has affected the world, the Lord's church and His people. The field prophet is aggressive, strong and powerful in will. Their approach to those in the field is like that of the navy seal. They are focused on the mission, blunt and tactical. They are fearless under the hand of the Lord. They come to make sure that the will of God is established, the covenant intact, and the system of the world affects his church. They come to turn the heart of the people back to the Lord. They understand this by these six points:

1. The Field prophet comes to release the Lord people from bondage.

""The Spirit of the LORD is upon Me, Because He has anointed Me To preach the gospel to the poor; He has sent Me to heal the brokenhearted, To proclaim liberty to the captives And recovery of sight to the blind, To set at liberty those who are oppressed; To proclaim the acceptable year of the LORD." Then He closed the book, and gave it back to the attendant and sat down. And the eyes of all who were in the synagogue were fixed on Him." (Luke 4:18-20 NKJV)

The Field prophet is relentless in its pursuit to make sure those in bondage are set free from the hand of the enemy. They are guarded in this pursuit and they want nothing more than to make sure the enemy has no place in the life of the Lord's people. The field prophet must understand this pursuit, if they are to carry out the assignment of the field prophet. Today's field prophet must be diligent in learning how the anointing of the goes beyond where they are currently, and into the depths and darkest of broken places.

2. The Field Prophet comes to deal with the world systems?

"So the LORD said to Moses: "See, I have made you as God to Pharaoh, and Aaron your brother shall be your prophet. You shall speak all that I command you. And Aaron your brother shall tell Pharaoh to send the children of Israel out of his land. And I will harden Pharaoh's heart, and multiply My signs and My wonders in the land of Egypt. But Pharaoh will not heed you, so that I may lay My hand on Egypt and bring My armies and My people, the children of Israel, out of the land of Egypt by great judgments. And the Egyptians shall know that I am the LORD, when I stretch out My hand on

Egypt and bring out the children of Israel from among them." (Exodus 7:1-5 NKJV)

The systems of this world have created havoc on the Lord's people and set in place systems with built debt, broken images and false popularity and fame. These systems pulled the people away from the Lord and help build the kingdom of darkness. The field prophet enters the world to deal with such systems and help break these systems so the Lord's people can become free. The field prophet will become aggressive, antagonistic and strained as they deal with such systems. They will leave no stone unturned until the assignment is done.

3. The Field Prophet comes to deal With the Broken Covenant.

"So Ahab sent for all the children of Israel, and gathered the prophets together on Mount Carmel. And Elijah came to all the people, and said, "How long will you falter between two opinions? If the LORD is God, follow Him; but if Baal, follow him." But the people answered him not a word. Then Elijah said to the people, "I alone am left a prophet of the LORD; but Baal's prophets are four hundred and fifty men. Therefore let them give us two bulls; and let them choose one bull for themselves, cut it in pieces, and lay it on the wood, but put no fire under it; and I will prepare the other bull, and lay it on the wood, but put no fire under it. Then you call on the name of your gods, and I will call on the name of the LORD; and the God who answers by fire, He is God." So all the people answered and said, "It is well spoken." Now Elijah said to the prophets of Baal, "Choose one bull for yourselves and prepare it first, for you are many; and call on the name of your god, but put no fire under it. " So they took the bull, which was given them, and they prepared it, and called on the name of Baal from morning even till noon, saying, "O Baal, hear us!" But there was no voice; no one answered. Then they leaped about the altar which they had

made. And so it was, at noon, that Elijah mocked them and said, "Cry aloud, for he is a god; either he is meditating, or he is busy, or he is on a journey, or perhaps he is sleeping and must be awakened." So they cried aloud, and cut themselves, as was their custom, with knives and lances, until the blood gushed out on them. And when midday was past, they prophesied until the time of the offering of the evening sacrifice. But there was no voice; no one answered, no one paid attention. Then Elijah said to all the people, "Come near to me." So all the people came near to him. And he repaired the altar of the LORD that was broken down. And Elijah took twelve stones, according to the number of the tribes of the sons of Jacob, to whom the word of the LORD had come, saying, "Israel shall be your name." Then, with the stones he built an altar in the name of the LORD; and he made a trench around the altar large enough to hold two seahs of seed. And he put the wood in order, cut the bull in pieces, and laid it on the wood, and said, "Fill four waterpots with water, and pour it on the burnt sacrifice and on the wood." Then he said, "Do it a second time," and they did it a second time; and he said, "Do it a third time," and they did it a third time. So the water ran all around the altar; and he also filled the trench with water. And it came to pass, at the time of the offering of the evening sacrifice, that Elijah the prophet came near and said, " LORD God of Abraham, Isaac, and Israel, let it be known this day that You are God in Israel and I am Your servant, and that I have done all these things at Your word. Hear me, O LORD, hear me, that this people may know that You are the LORD God, and that You have turned their hearts back to You again." Then the fire of the LORD fell and consumed the burnt sacrifice, and the wood and the stones and the dust, and it licked up the water that was in the trench. Now when all the people saw it, they fell on their faces; and they said, "The LORD, He is God! The LORD, He is God!" And Elijah said to them, "Seize the prophets of Baal! Do not let one of them escape!" So they seized them; and Elijah brought them down to the

Brook Kishon, and executed them there." (I Kings 18:20-40 NKJV)

When the covenant is broken, those who are a part of the covenant have lost their way. They become focused on wanting what they want and disconnected from the Lord altogether. They seek a false prophetic voice that will help them change such direction. The field prophet comes to deal with the enemy of the covenant and goes to war so the covenant stays intact. They go to war with words of those prophetic voices that would dare cause the Lord people to believe in a lie. Their whole purpose at that moment is to make sure that the people understand the divine covenant. At this moment the wisdom and knowledge of the divine heart of the Lord will be on display as the field prophet destroys the principality of the covenant.

4. The Field Prophet turns the heart of the people back to the Lord.

"Then he said to the multitudes that came out to be baptized by him, "Brood of vipers! Who warned you to flee from the wrath to come? Therefore bear fruits worthy of repentance, and do not begin to say to yourselves, 'We have Abraham as our father.' For I say to you that God is able to raise up children to Abraham from these stones. And even now the ax is laid to the root of the trees. Therefore every tree which does not bear good fruit is cut down and thrown into the fire."(Luke 3:7-9 NKJV)

The heart of salvation is the prophet's heart. He or she enters the field to bring redemption to those who are lost and misguided. They understand that their mantle is created in the redemptive blood of Christ. They seek to change the heart of the people by preaching a message of repentance. They look for fruit from those who have heard their message and rebuke those who would dare opposes it. Their job when it is all said in done, is to make sure the cross is the center of their prophetic assignment.

5. The Field Prophet brings healing and restoration to the Lord's people.

"God anointed Jesus of Nazareth with the Holy Spirit and with power, who went about doing good and healing all who were oppressed by the devil, for God was with Him." (Acts 10:38 NKJV)

The field prophet enters the field to bring healing and restoration to those who have been afflicted physically, mentally and spiritually. Their mantle sees beyond the brokenness of the body, mind and spirit and sees the healing in those who need it. Jesus brought healing to the masses and restores those things that were lost. This is the field prophet's assignment. This is a part of their destiny.

6. The Field Prophet comes to intercede for the city.

"Now as He drew near, He saw the city and wept over it, saying, "If you had known, even you, especially in this your day, the things that make for your peace! But now they are hidden from your eyes. For days will come upon you when your enemies will build an embankment around you, surround you and close you in on every side, and level you, and your children within you, to the ground; and they will not leave in you one stone upon another, because you did not know the time of your visitation.""
(Luke 19:41-44 NKJV)

When the field prophet enters the field, they are assigned to cities and place that have been covered with the spirit of darkness. They come to destroy the principalities over those cities and shift them into divine purpose. They come with intercession in their belly. They don't leave until the city has been captured by the spirit of God. The moment that prophet enters the city, the demonic influences that have set up siege in those cities tremble at the coming of the prophet. For they know that once the prophet comes into the city, the city comes to light.

As we conclude this chapter I hope you have learned the most important points of your placement. The truth is every experience is different, but every placement is not. The experiences at these placements will reveal your training, it will reveal your sacrifice, it will reveal your passion. You will be test above your limits; you will see personalities and conflict you will feel not in your control. But what matter is your ability to not lose yourself. Understand that your placement reflects who you are. You were born for this. To see the governments, temples, and the fields change. That change begins in your mantle. Remember that your placement does not define you, you define it.

CHAPTER SIX

The Activation of the Prophet

The word activation is defined as, making active; cause to function or act. The ministry of the prophet must be taken seriously as we evolve in the 21st century. And it must start with the immaturity of activating prophets to soon. A young prophet must prove himself or herself to handle the mantle of the prophet. This is the reason for training, because training exposes the life and depth of the person called to walk in the prophetic office. Activating a prophet before their time causes pain to those that they are called to. As the young prophet has not proven himself or herself to handle the lives of those the Lord has sent them to. The reality of this has come to the brink as prophets of today have come forth with little responsibility of the prophetic office. They have forsaken the process of the office to be popular and famous speakers. Those who activate such prophets must understand that they are responsible for those prophets. Activation of the prophetic is for those who have learned the office, and for those who understand the importance of the prophetic utterances inside their mouths. These prophets are proven students.

When activation has taken place the young prophet understands the responsibility of their mantle and what that mantle means to the Lord's people. The lead prophet that takes upon a group of prophets or a young prophet understands that activation is for those who yield to the process and have allowed themselves to be pruned by the hand of the Lord. Activation never happens until the young prophet has displayed the eight traits listed below. If the young prophet has mastered these things, then the young prophet is ready to be activated.

The Eight Signs of the Prophet's Release

"And it came to pass, when the LORD was about to take up Elijah into heaven by a whirlwind, that Elijah went with Elisha from Gilgal. Then Elijah said to Elisha, "Stay here, please, for the LORD has sent me on to Bethel." But Elisha said, "As the LORD lives, and as your soul lives, I will not leave you!" So they went down to Bethel. Now the sons of the prophets who were at Bethel came out to Elisha, and said to him, "Do you know that the LORD will take away your master from over you today?" And he said, "Yes, I know; keep silent!" Then Elijah said to him, "Elisha, stay here, please, for the LORD has sent me on to Jericho." But he said, "As the LORD lives, and as your soul lives, I will not leave you!" So they came to Jericho. Now the sons of the prophets who were at Jericho came to Elisha and said to him, "Do you know that the LORD will take away your master from over you today?" So he answered, "Yes, I know; keep silent!" Then Elijah said to him, "Stay here, please, for the LORD has sent me on to the Jordan." But he said, "As the LORD lives, and as your soul lives, I will not leave you!" So the two of them went on. And fifty men of the sons of the prophets went and stood facing them at a distance, while the two of them stood by the Jordan. Now Elijah took his mantle, rolled it up, and struck the water; and it was divided this way and that, so that the two of them crossed over on dry ground. And so it was, when they had crossed over, that Elijah said to Elisha, "Ask! What may I do for you, before I am taken away from you?" Elisha said, "Please let a double portion of your spirit be upon me." So he said, "You have asked a hard thing. Nevertheless, if you see me when I am taken from you, it shall be so for you; but if not, it shall not be so. " Then it happened, as they continued on and talked, that suddenly a chariot of fire appeared with horses of fire, and separated the two of them; and Elijah went up by a whirlwind into

heaven. And Elisha saw it, and he cried out, "My father, my father, the chariot of Israel and its horsemen!" So he saw him no more. And he took hold of his own clothes and tore them into two pieces. He also took up the mantle of Elijah that had fallen from him, and went back and stood by the bank of the Jordan. Then he took the mantle of Elijah that had fallen from him, and struck the water, and said, "Where is the LORD God of Elijah?" And when he also had struck the water, it was divided this way and that; and Elisha crossed over. Now when the sons of the prophets who were from Jericho saw him, they said, "The spirit of Elijah rests on Elisha." And they came to meet him, and bowed to the ground before him." (II Kings 2:1-15 NKJV)

The lead prophets training the young prophets have spent numerous of hours, days, months and years preparing the young prophets to take center stage of the prophetic office. The relationship in which the young prophet and his protégé have built should be one of great harmony, love and respect. The lead prophet has set an example of strength, courage and endurance. They have tested the young prophets' hearts and the endurance of their mantle. They have imparted everything he or she has known about the prophetic and has prepared the young prophet to engage the enemies of the kingdom of God. For the lead prophet there is only one thing left before he or she activates the young prophet into the fullness of his or her office and that is making sure that the young prophet understands eight major things. These eight things the lead prophet should look for before he or she activates and releases the young prophet into the fullness of the prophetic office:

1. The prophet's ability to sacrifice

We discuss sacrifice much in this literary work, so not surprisingly, when the lead prophet is ready to release the young prophet. The young prophet should have displayed the ability to sacrifice in any season. The lead prophet should not be ready to release the young prophet if the young prophet has not proven he or she can sacrifice. Sacrifice is important to the journey and season of the prophet. Understanding this will show the prophet's commitment to the heart of God.

2. The prophet's ability to hear instructions

The lead prophet in this second point looks to see how well the young prophet hears and follows instructions. The necessity of this again is to make sure that the young prophet understand order and fulfilling the assignment of the Lord the way it was given. This means the young prophet will be tested constantly in his or her last stage of development as they prove to the lead prophet they are ready to do what the Lord has called them to do.

3. The prophet's discipline

The young prophet must prove that he or she is disciplined in their flesh and how to handle the spirit of the prophet. The lead prophet looks for these two disciplines, since they are important to the young prophet's growth. If the young prophet is discipline in these two areas, it will display that the young prophet will not waiver in what was taught to him or her concerning their prophetic mantle. The young prophet will have a sense of value. They will prove that their consecration is more important than the things of this world. It is in discipline the lead prophet will see the fruit of the process and development of the prophet in which we talked about in the previous chapters.

4. The prophet's ability to serve

The lead prophet in this point will look for the young prophet's ability to walk in humility and understand it. The young prophet pride should have been killed through the years of process and development. Over the years and months they should have proven to the lead prophet that the church and the Lord's people are the most important thing to them. They have proven to forsake the limelight and understand that the greatness of their mantle is a towel in their hands. If the young prophet has not understood this, then the young prophet must repeat the process and the development stage.

5. The prophet's ability to understand honor

The young prophet over the years is taught honor and the lead prophet would place the young prophet in a situation that would give the young prophet the opportunity to show that honor. The lead prophet would make note of how the young prophet dealt with him and other leaders in times of adversity and other circumstances that would display the prophet's heart of honor. If the young prophet has not proven himself/ herself in the manner of honor, then the young prophet has shown the lead prophet, he or she does not have the ability to protect the anointing on the lives of the people of the Lord's church and those called to lead it. For no prophet can be activated and released until they learn the lesson of honor.

6. The prophet's ability to be a student

The young prophet's heart should have displayed a level of humility that has moved him or her into the seat of the student. The young prophet should have displayed in his or her training they can be teachable. The lead prophet understands the importance of the young prophet becoming a student because the prophetic office is always evolving. The constant revelation being released is important to the prophet's ministry. For this reason the seat of the student must be the heart of the young prophet in everything they do. The young prophet shows the lead prophet that he/she is teachable by learning and understanding and implementing everything that has been taught. The young prophet shows their eagerness to learn about the office and spends the necessary time in prayer learning the ins and outs of the spirit realm. The young prophet is never satisfied and always hungers to learn more about our Lord, the church, the Lord's people and their office.

7. The prophet's ability to understand warfare

The lead prophet looks to see if the young prophet understands the spirit of darkness. The young prophet over their years of training should have experience levels of warfare that would have proven their ability to fight against the kingdom of darkness. The young prophet during this stage should show their knowledge of the kingdom of darkness and a strategic plan to help combat what the enemy is doing in the season in which the warfare is presented. The young prophet must be able to show the spirit of a warrior and the heart to execute a kingdom assault against the dark forces of the enemy.

8. Your ability to interpret and teach the word of God.

The lead prophet must be able to see the young prophet's ability to exegete and teach the word of God. This is critical as the transformation of the church and the Lord's people depend on it. If the young prophet cannot do this, then he or she has displayed their inability to understand what the Lord is saying prophetically in His word. The word of God for the prophet must be the very thing he or she has learned under the prophetic office. Their study habits over the years of training should prove their theological and ideological outlook. The young prophet should be able to stand before the lead prophet and explain the word of the Lord and why he or she believes what they believe in. If the young prophet cannot do this, then they must return to the Table of the Lord.

These eight traits of the prophetic release symbolize something special about the young prophet. It says that he or she is ready to take upon the office that they spent years being processed. These eight traits state that they are ready for the mandate before them. The prophetic release speaks of the beginning of a legacy for the young prophet and how that legacy is defined by the strength and character of that young prophet's ability to understand and implement everything that has been taught. The young prophet is now ready to begin the journey of the prophetic office as they now hold the keys to the heart of God.

THE CONCLUSION

In closing The Prophet's Anatomy, Vol 2. My prayer is that you have come to an understanding on where you stand in the prophetic office. As you grow and learn who you are and what it means to walk in this office, I hope the Prophet's Anatomy becomes a tool for you to help you process this office in its fullness. What we must realize as we gather ourselves to understand the prophetic office, let us be reminded that the Prophetic office is the office that will help grow the church and shift it to its next level.

No more should this office be one of manipulation and greed. But one that seeks to establish the kingdom of God here on earth as it is in heaven. We have been chosen to unlock the revelation of the Lord and be an instrument to propel the Lord's people to their destiny. There is nothing more important in this season than becoming prophets of righteousness. The world is in need for you to finish the process, accept the call, and be ready to establish the word of the Lord. Allow the prophet inside you to rise up. Allow your Anatomy to speak the life of the prophet.

REFERENCE PAGE

1. All scripture have been taken from the NIV and New King James Bible.

2. Some definitions have been taken from Webster Dictionary. www.mw1.meriamwebster.com
3. www.thefreedictionary.com
4. www.dictionary.reference.com
5. Tyndale Bible Dictionary, Walter A. Elwell, Ph.D. and Philip W. Comfort, Ph.D., Tyndale House Publishers Wheaton Illinois.
6. Holman Illustrated Bible Dictionary, Trent C. Butler, Nashville Tennessee.
7. Nelson's New Illustrated Bible Dictionary, Ronald F. Youngblood, Thomas Nelson Publishers, 1995, 1986.
8. The Prophet's Dictionary, Paula A. Price, Ph.D., Whitaker House.

Made in the USA
Columbia, SC
10 July 2022

63249662R00055